SERMON SEEDS

Sermon Seeds

40 Creative Sermon Starters

Dottie Escobedo-Frank

Abingdon Press
Nashville

SERMON SEEDS: 40 Creative Sermon Starters

Library of Congress Cataloging-in-Publication Data

Escobedo-Frank, Dottie.
  Sermon seeds : 40 creative sermon starters / Dottie Escobedo-Frank.
    p. cm.
  ISBN 0-687-33171-4
  1. Sermons—Outlines, syllabi, etc. 2. Bible—Sermons—Outlines, syllabi, etc. I. Title.

BV4223.E83 2005
251'.02—dc22   2005023658

06 07 08 09 10 11 12 13 14 — 10 09 08 07 06 05 04 03 02

MANUFACTURED IN THE UNITED STATES OF AMERICA

CONTENTS

For Abigail McLemore,
a chef of the most creative kind, an artiste of the palate, a lover of
all that is good and kind and courageous. For all you have endured
with strength and dignity, and for what we have learned by watch-
ing you tackle cancer at such a young age. This book is dedicated to
you because you are most beloved.

For Steve Marshall,
the pastor who first showed me about creativity and sermons. This
book is dedicated to you because you paved the way.

For Cliff Wright,
the musical genius who listens well and transfers my thoughts into
music that goes beyond the limitations of words. This book is dedi-
cated to you because you are my partner in ministry.

For Lisa Burgess,
the creative guru who sees the world in pictures of grace and good-
ness. This book is dedicated to you because you carry the seeds of
innovation in your soul.

For Jan Brophy,
the woman who organizes my messes, knows my quirks, and still
hangs in. For taking the jumbled bits and bringing order and
understanding and clarity. This book is dedicated to you because
you always make me laugh.

For my creative family:
Mom, Dad, Lee, Allan, Cherie, Sarita, and Mando.
For loving me while knowing me so well. For being my soul mates
and my most treasured friends. This book is dedicated to you
because your ingenuity astounds me.

For my family: Jim, Sara, Natalie, and Andrew.
You know I couldn't do life without you. You are my warm blan-
ket, my favorite jeans, and my best cup of coffee. This book is dedi-
cated to you because I love you with my whole heart.

And, for Jesus, Lover of my soul.

INTRODUCTION

I love surprises! As a little girl, I did my best to bring surprise into my life and into the lives of my family. I remember one day my big sister Cherie was doing dishes when I decided to have some fun. I went outside and quietly snuck back in through the front door, hiding behind the corner. As soon as I heard Cherie coming my way, I jumped out and screamed at the top of my lungs. Cherie was totally shocked, and her automatic reaction was a quick and firm slap to my face! Ouch! But I was not done yet. After a hug and some laughter, I went outside again and snuck back in through the front door. I hid until the right moment, and—you guessed it—I jumped out and scared her one more time with my horrendous scream. This time she had a metal bucket in her hand and, without thinking, she bopped me across the arm with that bucket. She was laughing, and I was crying! It was the best of fun, and I look back on that moment with fondness and chuckle at my stupidity!

In junior high, my friend Clarissa "fainted" in our teacher's arms, only to shout out, "April Fools'!" after she was scooped up and carried toward the door. Thank goodness the math teacher had a keen sense of humor! Once Clarissa even convinced my boyfriend that he should go out with her, and all the while I was hiding on the floor of the backseat of the car. Poor Danny! Clarissa is in heaven now, and I have no doubt that she is giving the angels a good laugh. My sister Sarita and I would often trade places on the phone, pretending we were each other to find out what was really going on! April Fools' Day is my favorite holiday because it is a day when surprises are expected. Ask my last church what fun Sunday can be on April Fools' Day!

Sermons have a reputation in recent history of being boring—things people "endure." When I went to seminary, the thing I dreaded most about becoming a pastor was that I'd have to give sermons. I was scared to death of getting up in front of people, but also, I was not excited about watching people fall asleep at my expense! I was determined to find a way to make this part of ministry fun! So I began my own personal search for something (I didn't know exactly what) that would bring surprise and delight to the church once a week.

After I had been a pastor for a few years, delivering my fair share of "yawners," I attended an evangelism conference at Community Church of Joy in Glendale, Arizona. I was fascinated as I watched the staff weave together word, technology, and fabulous music to create a worship experience that kept me on the edge of my seat, straining to hear every word. Excited, I began to wonder if I could do the same thing in my little church down the road.

No more than two or three days after the conference, I was sitting in my office as mad as a hornet. I realized I couldn't do what they did at Community Church of Joy. We didn't have the technology, the money, or the staff to support any creative ideas I might come up with. But I stopped myself from developing a defeatist attitude and began to think of creative venues that did not cost money. I recalled the world of the arts: painting, sculpture, poetry, and song. I thought about mime, dance, drama, and interviews. I remembered my dad's comment, "Poverty is the genius of invention, Dottie." I began to realize that creativity doesn't require money but that it does require out-of-the-box surprises. I began to experiment. I began to surprise myself and others. I began to think of sermons in a new way.

Sermons are creative avenues for God's message. Every week pastors work hand in hand with God to create a structure for the delivery of an old, old story. The problem is that we need to tell that story in a new, new way. Most pastors did not take "Creative Dance" or "Drama" or "Visual Arts" classes in seminary, so we lack the understanding of delivery needed to reach this generation and beyond. The old, old way of delivering sermons (a manuscript monologue) has to decrease, and a new format must emerge. The language has changed. Multimedia replaces print. "Multi" replaces "uni"-form. Sermon giving becomes like a multifaceted diamond: many sides to the same jewel. We are at a place in history where personal learning is at an all-time high. What we learned in seminary is the foundation, but the walls and the roof will not go up without further exploration of this new language.

To complicate the problem further, most churches are small, understaffed entities of one or two. How does a small church with a solo pastor and a part-time assistant begin to find resources to "produce" a sermon every week? Most pastors have attended conferences in which they see the fabulous way the message is enhanced by a staff of twenty and by multimedia equipment. When they return home, they are faced with their own reality: a pastor, an assistant, and not a whit of the latest technical support. Discouragement is common after attending such events.

There is an answer! Creative, multifaceted sermons can happen without extravagant resourcing! It takes *more* creativity and *more* "outside-the-box" thinking, but it *can* happen in a small church. This book is intended to stir your creative juices within the boundaries of your own reality and to remind you that everything does not boil down to finances! God made us as creative beings! So as you read the outlines of sermon ideas, let your imagination flow, use whatever bits and pieces you need from this book, and build upon the creativity that has been offered to you in these pages.

I am admittedly a novice in the areas of pastoring, sermonizing, and creative arts. But being a novice has its advantages. After all, novices are more willing to risk failure. Find your areas of newness, tap into the Creative Genius of All Time, and have the fun of your life!

Happy storytelling!

CHAPTER ONE

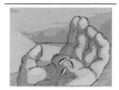

CREATIVE SERMONS

JEREMIAH: THE CREATIVE PROPHET

Creative sermons are not new. In fact, they are as old as they come! It started with creativity in worship (something we must also learn from, btw!). In Genesis we see the first musician, Jubal, who is the ancestor of all who play the harp and the flute (see Gen. 4:21). The artistry of the Ark of the Covenant and the Tabernacle, and the craftwork of Bezalel and Oholiab, is described in great detail in Exodus 25–31. King David brought music and dance to the people, bringing the soul's language to the forefront of worship. Solomon worshiped in the creations of fabulous architecture. Isaiah used vivid imagery to get his message across (e.g., in Isaiah 31:5, God is compared to an angry bird). And Jeremiah brought it all together to become "the Creative Prophet." (Most remember him as "the Weeping Prophet," but there's more to old Jeremiah than that!)

Jeremiah, if we really look at him, was a rather outrageous fellow. A priest and a prophet in Judah, he spoke to five kings of his day (Josiah, Jehoahaz, Jehoiakim, Jehoiachin, and Zedekiah) and three different empires (Judah, Babylon, and Egypt). He was an emotional guy, not holding back on the feelings that come when living for God. He spoke messages of hope for transformation from the doom and gloom, wishing God would occasionally give him a kinder message. It was the doom and gloom that got him in trouble. He made many enemies because of his harsh words. He was thrown in prison many times, taken to a foreign country against his will, and probably died in Egypt, far from his beloved homeland. He was a writer who used prose, poetry, parable, lament, biography, and history. The Hebrew title for the book of Lamentations is "How," which is a guttural cry of grief.[1]

Against that backdrop, I want to point out how creative Jeremiah was in getting across the awful and wonderful messages of his day. He describes the terror from the north as a "boiling pot," ready to boil over in anger (Jer. 1:13-16). He sees Israel following after other gods and says, "You are like a restless female camel, desperate for a male! You are like a wild donkey, sniffing the wind at mating time" (Jer. 2:23*b*–24*a*). He moves on to more concrete metaphors when he illustrates how Judah's pride affects their relationship with God by burying a linen belt in the Euphrates River. When the belt was dug up, it was mildewed, falling apart, and really useless (Jer. 13:1–14). He is taken down to the potter's house, and God speaks to him through the work of the potter (Jer. 18:1–10). He smashes a clay jar at the Potsherd Gate to illustrate how the people would be shattered by their sin (Jer. 19). In chapter 24, Jeremiah describes a vision of how God would deal with the good and the bad in the same way we deal with good figs (useful to feed and well received) and bad figs (rotten and rejected). He gives a message of submission to the rule of the Babylonians (Jer. 27–28) by living his life while wearing an ox yoke (some heavy babies for sure!). Jeremiah buys a piece of land, obtains the deed of purchase, and hands it to Baruch in the presence of the people, asking that he keep it in a pottery jar where it will be well preserved. This is the message of hope that God will someday bring the people back from Babylon to the place where they can buy and sell property, houses, and vineyards in their own land (Jer. 32). And at Tahpanhes, Jeremiah gathers together the people and buries large stones between the rocks at the entrance to Pharaoh's palace as a concrete description of the way God would let the Babylonians have control over Egypt (Jer. 43:8–13).[2]

Jeremiah had a message to tell, and he wanted it to be so memorable and vivid that the people would hear it and be transformed. He wanted the words to change hearts and ways so that the people would return to God. And that is our place in history. We have a message to tell, but not many are listening. Perhaps one part of our problem is that we are not memorable enough.

It was Jeremiah's passion for the lost people of his tribe that brought him to a place of willingness to be used by God in these unusual ways. And it is our passion for the lost of our communities that causes us to look at the delivery forms of our message.

GOD THE CREATOR

> *So God created people in his own image; God patterned them after himself; male and female he created them. (Gen. 1:27)*

We were created in God's image, in the image of the Creator of the universe. It boggles my mind to think that I was created in God's image, but the part that is most amazing is that I was created to be creative. When I was a young girl, I used to think that I was the one in the family who missed out on the creative genes. My mom could write and recite poetry and stories, my dad could fix anything out of nothing, and I had sisters who could paint and dance and brothers who could write and make things work. But I couldn't see my own creativity. So when I began to look at doing sermons creatively, I felt out of my league. I tell you this only to present you with the idea that you are creative even if you don't know that about yourself yet. After all, you were made in the image of the Creator! You might have to do some digging to find the ways you can be creative, but I can assure you that you won't have to dig far. It might be just below the surface of your self-understanding.

Look at what our Creator God did! God made the universe and the stars and set the planets in motion and timed things according to the moon's cycle. God put a whole bunch of water in the boundaries of sand and gave it a back-and-forth motion. God made a world where raindrops have different sounds and snow falls in silence. He made the earth freeze over with icicles and melt with the warmth of the sun. God set the colors of green and brown and blue as the backdrop so that we could also experience the reds and yellows and purples and oranges of the world. God made a way for green things to receive chlorophyll and water and air. He made the deepest caverns and the tallest mountains, and he made the snakelike rivers to connect the dots in between. God breathed life into babies and elephants and kangaroos. God gave emotions to connect humans and animals. God created music! He gave us sensory knowledge, and the love of beauty and order and the desire for peace. We are made in the image of this kind of Creator.

So think about it . . . there's got to be something of the creative spirit within you. I want to encourage you to find it and to develop it and to make room for it. I want you to get out of your boxes and circles and ruts and find out about the rest of the world out there. And I want you to apply all that you have learned to your creation of sermons. I will give you a few ideas on how to get started in this book, but they really are elementary, and I believe that your creations will far exceed mine. The ideas presented here are really jumping-off places. They are ideas to get your own creative juices flowing in your unique style. Feel free to imitate, mix-up, re-create, and totally redo any idea that you take from these pages. This book is an idea book—a book that you can use to start to see things a new way.

ELEMENTS OF CREATIVITY

What I learned over time and through much trial and error is that there are some recognizable patterns of creativity. These elements of creativity are building blocks that can help you grow in sermonizing. Look at them, and see how many forms you can use to create a message. Note: it's best to use one or two in a message . . . don't resort to overkill!

1. **Surprise** What a delight it is in life to be surprised. Some of the best sermons I remember hearing are ones where I was surprised by the ending or by something in the middle. The surprise caught me off guard and made me sit up and listen. It reminds me of the saying "Made ya look!" That's what surprises do. See if you can find ways to initiate surprise into the body of your message, and see how intently people listen after you do!

2. **Distraction** When we draw attention away from a problem, we have a second chance at the problem. Often this second chance is what helps us to view Scripture in a new way or to see applications to our lives that we can't get when we doggedly pursue a solution. Try the distractions of stories that don't end until later, of implementing something that seems irrelevant, or of looking away and then looking back at something. It brings a newness to the sermon that will give you a smile.

3. **Imaging** To image is to make visible. We can do this with descriptive words, or we can actually bring an image to the people and

let the image speak for itself. For example, when talking about baggage, have a pile of suitcases up on the stage that provides a visual response beyond anything words could ever say (see Nine Seeds). Pictures are worth more than words, so include images in new and old ways.

4. **Metaphor** Metaphors are connectors linking ideas that otherwise might not be seen together. We have a rich history of ascribing metaphors to God. "God's hands" is a metaphor that connects God's actions with our understanding of touch. Jesus was a master at using metaphors, similes, and parables, and we can be masters at the art of description as well. Don't get stuck in old metaphors though. Find metaphors that have not been used before, and surprise people with a depth of thought that is relevant to our cultural understanding of the world.

5. **Remix** Look at things and mix them up in new ways. When we get good at cooking, we can use basic ingredients and throw in a few extra spices or tastes to change the outcome. One of my favorite surprise tastes was at a chili cook-off where one contestant put chocolate into the chili. It changed the texture and the taste, and it influenced the spices already in the mix. I never forgot that one. That's the point.[3]

6. **Layering** To layer a sermon is to add one element, then gradually add another, and then another. For example, before you begin talking, show a silent picture of the story, say, of Jesus riding into Jerusalem on Palm Sunday. Then add music without words to the picture, and then music with words, inviting the people to join in the song. Then as the music and picture fade behind you, begin talking about the story. Layering helps people to go deeper with the meaning of the message. It starts at a safe place and then goes a little further in our understanding than we had planned.

7. **Sensory** Although we used to be a people who learned by hearing, most of us today are visual learners. If you notice, you can tell who the auditory learners are in your congregation. They are the ones who close their eyes to hear the sermon. Ask them why and you might hear about them listening to the radio in the same manner, or to music, etc. But visual learners are people who take in all kinds of information by what they see around them. Most of us are adept at visual cues and have been greatly influenced by the age of television and the Internet. If you want to add to the typical senses used in sermons, think about the sense of smell. Smell can take us back in time to a memory that is vivid. Think of the smell of home-

made cookies, or the smell of freshly baked bread. The old traditions of the church included the sense of smell when they used incense as a way to welcome the presence of God. Taste is also a memory connector. When we taste the Communion elements, we remember the giving of Christ for our sins. The sense of touch involves cells that cover the whole body. Touch communicates warmth, caring, and connection. Touching a shoulder, for example, tells someone that you are with her. It provides tactile memory that touches our emotions. Therefore, any time that you can add the sensory communication, you will enhance the experience of worship.

8. **Play** Play includes humor, fun, and lighthearted activity. Many studies have shown the benefits of humor to our overall health. Joy is good for the soul. The thing about playfulness and humor is that it lets us look sideways at an idea. We laugh at something and take it lightly, and then we can zero in on the serious side of the same subject. It opens us up to the possibilities that we previously shunned. For too long, we've given ourselves to the thought that church is only a serious endeavor. But it is more than that. A lighthearted approach to the world and to the subject matter may enable you to go deeper than you ever imagined. That's why we know intuitively that laughter and tears go hand in hand.[4]

9. **Connecting the Circle** I often use this technique to bring back a theme or story or to end up where I started. For example, I may begin to tell a story, then go off into other sequences of thought, and finish the sermon with the end of the story I started in the beginning. Follow that? It's an easy but effective way to bring a point to a conclusion. It leaves the hearer with that feeling of having gone "full circle" with a topic. It adds completeness to the message.

10. **Interruption** To stop and start a message can be effective because it makes a topic lighter in order to go deeper. When we are interrupted, we forget what we were doing, and when we get back to the task, we often have a new take on it. So too with interruptions. Plan interruptions in your message. I have done messages with "musical hats" (see Three Seeds) and with plain old interruptions by cued laypeople (see Seven Seeds). These are surprising and cause people to pay closer attention to what lies ahead.

11. **Musical** The musical sermon is one of my favorite forms to work with because the possibilities are endless. I started using these by talking to Cliff Wright, the worship director, and giving him ideas for the message. He would talk to me about songs that worked the metaphor, and we would go back and forth between word and

song in a planned and seamless way. This takes practice and trust between the two giving the message, but is well worth the effort. Once, a harpist worked with me on a message, providing musical backdrops to the words and spaces for reflection in the message. Don't be afraid to use snatches of secular as well as sacred sounds.

12. **Artistic** The arts are a wonderful way to communicate a message. Think of ways that you can mix dance, mime, painting, sculpting, weaving, drama, and even cooking into a sermon. The first time I heard about a creative sermon was when I served in my first church. The pastor who preceded me, Rev. Steve Marshall, had delivered a sermon with no words and a little music, as he painted a picture of Jesus on canvas before the very eyes of the congregation. It was so memorable that the church hailed it as "the best sermon ever," and that painting still hangs in the church. Artistic expression is valuable, and it is a form that has possibilities beyond the scope of these pages. Let your artistic imagination run wild!

FINDING THE OBVIOUS

In the church, we have delineated between the "clergy" and the "laity" for so long that we have forgotten we are really more a *collective* group of people than a *separate* group of people. That is what the phrase "priesthood of all believers" is all about. But when it comes to sermons, we have maintained our distinctions. What I'd like for us to consider is how the laity and clergy can form sermons together for the next generation. In fact, I call that combining of resources "claity," because it describes the way clergy and laity are one. We are connected as clay, and to separate us too much only minimizes our strength and mass.

So find what you've got in your congregation. Find the artists, the musicians, the technicians, and the firefighters. Ask them how they would interpret certain scriptures that involve their craft. Get their advice and ask them to help form a message. You will be surprised at the new things you'll discover when you ask the experts in the fields to be your guide.

WILLING TO FAIL

It will happen. Failure is a sure thing in creative messaging, so if this is something you can't do, then just regift this book to someone else right now. I remember feeling like a fool more than once. I have had to get back up and do-over more times than I'd like to admit. But things get smoother as we learn from our failures. Bigger patterns of what works in the art of communication emerge. Our understanding of what works is heightened by what doesn't work. Don't be afraid to fail. Just get up, dust off your britches, and get back at it.

REST

Creativity doesn't emerge from tired souls. It takes rest and space for a soul to create. My best advice to you as you begin this journey to create sermons is to first study the passage and get the main point firm in your mind. Then, forget about it for a while. Set it down and go do something fun, or do something that has nothing to do with church work. Some of the best ideas I get come while I am out jogging or gardening or following around my teenagers. It is when I forget about sermons that the ideas pop up. When you have an idea—a seed—write it down quickly before it slips away. Often the idea will directly relate to what your brain was working on before you went to play, and you will be delightfully surprised by what comes to you. Most creative people know the secret that it takes rest to be able to do the work of creation.

NOTE TO WORSHIP TEAMS

In working with worship teams, remember to put first things first. Encourage them first to be worshipers: to come to the worship moment with their whole hearts and souls, laying aside the work of worship to just worship. As we lead in worship, we must first be worshipers. Next, encourage your team to pray for worship. Pray that they will be protected from things that draw us away from worshiping God, and pray that the people will come ready to meet God in community. Pray for the sacrifice of praise to be acceptable and honorable to God. And finally, plan well ahead for the worship moment. When we do the work of planning well, we can do all that is possible and then set it aside and worship God. It is when we don't plan well that we spend the worship hour worrying about the details instead of meeting God. Plan and prepare so that you can set aside worry and be in God's presence.

WORD OF WARNING!

Worship the Creator, not the creativity. The one hesitation I have in writing this book is that it can become a manual of form alone. We cannot become so enamored with our creativity that we worship it. No! We worship *God* and offer our creativity as an expression of our love for God. Let's draw the line in the sand well so that we don't step over into the area of idolatry of form. For that reason, I don't recommend doing creative sermons every week. Most times we just need to talk to the people straight from the heart. Then seed your sermons with creativity as you feel the need. These are not tricks to learn. They are only tools for expression. Worship the Creator *with* your creativity.

CHAPTER TWO

BACKDROPS

As a deer pants for streams of water,
so I long for you, O God. (Ps. 42:1)

CORPORATE WORSHIP

Breathing is hard to explain because it is first nature to us. It's something we hardly ever think about. We can describe breathing as a movement of air in and out of our bodies, and we know that it supplies life-giving oxygen to our blood. So while it serves as a vital life-function, we hardly notice breath when it serves us well. If breathing becomes difficult due to illness, panic, or extreme exercise, then we think about it. But we don't normally think about breath because it is such a natural part of life. We think about it only when it is missing.

Worship is like breathing. We can describe the movements of worship and the forms of worship that have developed through history and tradition. We know when worship is *not* happening and when our form of worship is *not* connecting to our souls. But because God created us to pant after Him and to worship Him as first nature, it is sometimes hard to put words to the moments of connection that we call "worship."

We have a rich history of falling forward on our faces to worship God. And in the Bible we can see how the people who were followers of God sought to worship in their own contexts and in ways that made sense to them. We can look at recent history and classify worship as "traditional" or "contemporary," and now as "emerging" or "postmodern." Different forms of worship make sense to different people. But when we strip away the form, we are still falling forward before God with heart, mind, body, and soul. We are still humbling ourselves before our Creator, remembering who we are and who He is, as we become comfortable in our natural position of "created." We are still, no matter what form we name, praising the Creator above all else, worshiping only one God, and adoring the One who loves us enough to be present in our lives. God is still the One we cry out to when we end up in a heap of trouble.

Worship is remembering our position in life. It is remembering God. Worship is falling forward to kiss the One who gives us breath and life and hope.

Our souls pant for God, and the panting is like breathing. We were born for this kind of panting. It is a life-giving, hope-sustaining, toxin-removing movement of life that we can't even begin to explain.

TABERNACLE AND TEMPLE WORSHIP

Since the time of King Solomon, we have been engaged in Temple worship. While King David was building his own palace of splendor, it occurred to him that he was living better than the Lord was living in His "tent." So he planned a house of glory for the Lord, which was actually built by his son, King Solomon (see 2 Sam. 7). And so from that point on, people traveled to the Temple to worship God in a sacred spot or location. God resides in the Temple, and we go to meet God. Throughout the ages, we can see how that idea has continued. We "go to church." We "go and pray" at the church sanctuary. We "go" to gather, sing, hear the Word, and worship our God.

John Wesley was certainly raised in this form of worship. He believed that he was meant to preach in the churches and pulpits of his day. But there was a period in John's life when he was not reaching the people in the pews and was continually ostracized and asked *not* to come back to preach. He couldn't believe his ears. During this time, John's friend George Whitefield was having success preaching out in the fields of England. People were hearing the Good News and were responding with tremendous life-changing moments. It was a move of God in history that changed the church.

George was planning to be away for a weekend and asked his Anglican friend John to fill in at his "pulpit" in the fields. John responded with a firm "No!" reminding George that he was called to preach in the churches and not in the fields. George responded by reminding John that he was not having much success there! Then George twisted his request with a little guilt by saying something like, "If you don't preach, they won't hear." John preached to the people in the fields for the first time and was amazed at the way the Word was heard and at the overwhelming response of the people.

And so John Wesley used this approach again and again, taking church to the fields, the street corners, and the factories. In fact, he got so good at this that he sailed the seas, took the gospel to the frontier of new America, and birthed, quite by accident, the group of Christians called "Methodists."[5] All because he was willing to go beyond Temple worship.

I wonder if John Wesley went back to the Scripture and remembered Tent worship. The Tabernacle was also called the Tent of Meeting, because it was the place where God and the people of God met. In fact, the word *tabernacle* means "dwelling place." In Exodus 25:8 God spoke to Moses and said,

---

I want the people of Israel to build me a sacred residence where I can live among them.

The difference between Tabernacle worship and Temple worship[6] was that the Tent of God was portable and moved from place to place, depending on where the people were. You see, it was God's plan to go where the people went and to live in their presence. This is the God who seeks out you and me!

If we look at Exodus 40, we can see the movement of God and God's people. The people were so enamored with this God who dwelt among them that they came to follow God wherever God went. So, when the cloud by day and fire by night lifted from the Tabernacle and moved, the people packed up the Tent of Meeting and went on the road with God. This is the essence of transformation. It is the movement of finding the God who seeks us out and then following God wherever He goes because we long to dwell in that Presence. Because we want to be near Him. Because we need His breath, His life-giving words, and His direction. Because we love Him.

And so, I've been pondering that movement from Tabernacle worship (not worshiping the Tabernacle, but worshiping *in* the moveable Tent) to Temple worship (not worshiping the Temple, but worshiping *in* the located Temple). I've been noticing, as have countless others like yourself, that not many folk are coming to worship God in the "Temple" these days. And I've been wondering if we somehow need to get back to Tabernacle worship.

But in a new way. Like speaking in a way that reaches people in the streets and in the fields and in the world. Like working with others to pronounce the Good News in moveable ways. Like imagining a transportable gospel that goes to the places and the margins where people have not yet heard how much God loves them. I've been wondering . . .

STABLE FORCES

But when we go out into new territory, before we launch ahead, we must remember the stable forces—the things that we *don't change* in worship. If we forget to remember the stable forces, we will march ahead with much fear and trepidation. The stable forces are our foundations in worship that not only ground us in history and tradition but also keep us from losing touch with the community of saints who have gone before us. You may come up with your own set of "stable forces" that is better than what I've listed, and if so, good for you! For me, the stable forces that provide foundation are:

1. **Remembering Who God Is**
   The entrance to a worship gathering is designed to remember who God is. To remember God's love for us and to come to Him with praise and adoration as we recall all of His wonderful works. It is to put aside our own selves, to clear our thoughts and souls for a time as we focus on God our Father, the Holy Spirit our Sustainer, and Jesus our Redeemer. It is to look full in the face of our God. This moment of remembering and seeing God brings us to a place of humility, gratefulness, and unabashed adoration.

2. **Remembering Who We Are**
   As we see God face to face, we are brought to a place where we can look at ourselves with truth and honesty. In this moment of the worship gathering, we have confession, personal and corporate reflection, and creeds. We see ourselves, we take time to

reflect on God's love and forgiveness in our lives, and we allow God's transformational power of love to remake us and to reshape our present and future being. We open ourselves to be changed by this God who loves us fully.

3. Remembering God's Word

God's life-giving Word is proclaimed for all to hear. Proclamation may happen in different forms, but it is always based on the Scripture and interpreted through the grace of Jesus Christ. It is in the proclamation that God seals the transformation occurring in our lives. It is here that growth and fruit begin to be apparent in our lives. In proclamation, the Holy Spirit brings the power to begin again.

4. Responding to God

This part of the gathering may include space for personal or corporate response to meeting God in the gathering. It might involve personal prayer, acts of dedication, sacraments, offering, or reflection. It is the time that we listen deeper and move toward God because we recognize God's grace and power to transform.

5. Resending to God's World

Recognizing that we need reminders of our place of mission on a regular basis, we are resent to God's world at every gathering. We are commissioned, blessed, and challenged to take what was given to us and regift it to the rest of the world. We are reminded that the gift of God's love is not meant to be held in trust for a later date, but is meant to be freely given away so that others may know God's love and so that they too may gather to worship. Worship is natural to all of God's creations, as we live and breathe.

MOVEABLE FORCES

Once we determine the stable forces of worship, then we can find the places where we can travel—take worship on the road, so to speak. We do that with our foundations in place. The ways we can change include, but are certainly not limited to, the following:

1. Orders of Worship

We sometimes get stuck in a rut of doing the same thing the same way over and over again, just because it is easier. Even traditions that don't have a written "order of worship" may have fallen into a service that is similar week after week. While there needs to be familiarity for the people, it is sometimes good to mix up the order of worship. For example, what if on World Communion Sunday, you start the service celebrating Holy Communion? What if you start with the sermon and end with the singing? What if you put the offering in a different spot? Sometimes changing the order of things a bit can open up an element of surprise and can keep people attentive to what's going on in worship.

2. Forms

We love to worship forms. We have been committing that sin of idolatry for ages. Remember when Moses left the Israelites in Aaron's care while he went up the mountain? When he came down, he found that, in the absence of their leader, the people had found a way to worship a god they could see, which in this case was a golden calf. We haven't really stopped doing that even today. You know how it is. We like the cross to be placed on the altar just right, and if by chance it is moved to make room for the Communion elements or for some other art form that points to the message, then we have a—pardon the pun—cow! If the Communion elements are changed from wafers to loaves of bread or the method is changed from intinction to receiving by hand, the response is not often favorable. We've all received those notes left in the offering plate. We are habitual worshipers of form.

But we can teach ourselves and our people how to be free enough from form to experience worship in new ways. We can experience the fullness of worship through the views of artists, visual artists, dancers and so many others, as we open worship to being shaped by the talented leaders in our midst. Take a look at your forms. Value them. Expand them. Don't worship them.

3. Beginnings and Endings

Surprise beginnings to worship can bring an increased sense of awareness to the worship setting. And surprise endings can make people buzz about what happened when God met them during worship. Work with the beginnings and endings of worship times, and find ways to do a new thing every once in a while. Could you exchange the beginning and the ending? Could you end with praise and adoration and begin with the sending out? Could you encourage someone in the congregation to come up with the ending to worship? The possibilities are endless . . . and beginning-full. See what happens!

4. Atmosphere

The atmosphere of the worship setting has been underrepresented for quite some time now. It used to be of utmost concern. Think of the cathedrals in England, and you'll see how architecture and atmosphere go hand in hand. While our churches may not be made of marble or stained-glass windows, we can still do much to create an atmosphere for worship.

If worship is a way to become more intimate with God and with others, consider how your space prohibits or enhances that relationship. Are your pews set to look forward and upward (at God) but never in a way that enables people to see one another as well? How does your lighting enhance the setting as a place to approach your Maker? Do your sacred objects change enough to be noticed and to make a theological statement? Is your altar a space that tells the message of the gospel as much as the sermon?

One of my favorite places to experience atmosphere is Grace Community Church in Shreveport, Louisiana.[7] It is a simple building with well-placed artwork throughout the sanctuary. The baptistery is a flowing pond. The chairs are moveable and are often arranged in a semicircle where you can see the front of the worship space as well as see the people who come to worship. The altar is filled with visual art that depicts the theme of the message. You never know what you will see on the altar, and its design leads you to worship before the official start of the corporate worship time. If you step outside the door behind the altar, you will see a wonderfully-messy art room complete with all kinds of raw materials that are continuously being formed for worship. You will also see how that art room flows outside as some of the hardest work of worship is being done out on the lawn. It's an artist's workplace, and what you see behind the scenes is seen in all glory every week. The atmosphere at Grace Community prepares hearts and souls to meet God and to meet one another.

5. Expectations

The element of surprise is not to be underrated. While we are not interested in surprise merely for the sake of surprise, we recognize that surprise can open up the mind and heart to new ways of hearing God. Take what is "expected" in worship, and throw in a twist to see what happens.

At Mission Bell United Methodist Church in Glendale, Arizona, we totally changed the sanctuary for a Maundy Thursday service. We took out the chairs and put round tables in their place. A group of women set the tables with beautiful tablecloths and their family china. On each table we placed the Communion elements in the center, along with a bowl for handwashing. When people began arriving, many of them thought they had come at the wrong time because the setting was so different. But they sat down, watched a film, and heard a word. They shared some thoughts with those at their table, and then they served one another Communion.

It was an old tradition, set in an old way, and it surprised everyone. We remember that service with thankfulness for the way God met us as individuals and as a community.

6. <u>Community Connectors</u>

Many of us already understand that prayers and creeds are community connectors. There is something wonderful about saying the Lord's Prayer as a community of faith and hearing everyone pray together. I am an advocate of these "rote" connectors of faith. When I go to the hospital to pray for a family, there is an incredible sense of comfort when the family prays together, when they sing "Amazing Grace" together, or when they remember God together. It tells us, in a tangible way, that we are not alone. And that is a wonderful message to hear when we are in pain.

But we also need to be aware of teaching these "rote" words to the next generation. We may need to do so in different ways. For example, we could say the Apostles' Creed together with music layered underneath the words. Or we can sing "Amazing Grace" to a new beat, take it back to the "traditional" way of singing it, and then return to the new beat. Or, we can listen to the Lord's Prayer spoken overhead with harp music, pray the words together, and end by listening to harp music. While these methods require more work, the reward of teaching the faith community connectors to the next generation is invaluable and will last for an eternity.

These moveable forces are only the beginning of what can happen. We have not even started to look at ways to take our worship service (literally) out to the community. I believe that taking our worship beyond the walls of our buildings is where hope for our future lies.

FLOW AND THE HOLY SPIRIT—MAKING ROOM FOR GOD

On a less-than-regular basis I have dabbled in the art of jogging for exercise. While learning to jog, I read books that explain technique and form, and I learned about "flow." Flow is that moment when jogging becomes easy. Time fades away and you feel "in the flow" of the moment, unaware of your surroundings and totally at peace with the run and the road. This is the moment that all runners hope for amid the daily grind of pounding the trails and ticking off the miles. Runners describe the experience of flow as being able to run for miles without a sense of difficulty or effort.

I learned about flow in another arena as well. Musicians describe it as that moment when the music takes over, causing them to lose all sense of time and space and to feel they are being pulled along by the sound. Flow is also the way that musicians move from song to song without spaces of interruption. To keep a gig "in the flow" is to keep it moving along smoothly so that those who are listening don't know when the starts and stops occur.

The Holy Spirit comes to us in moments of flow. These are the times in worship when we forget the troubles and the trials and the self and the success; these are the moments when we experience God alone, unaware of the time passing or the daily tasks to which we must return.

As worship leaders, we can look at the ways we flow from one point in the service to the next and can see the whole service as a movement of loving God and neighbor. We can make sure the stops and starts within the service are not interrupting what God is communicating with the people and with us. We can pay attention to the flow by learning from the musicians and the runners . . . and by listening to the Holy Spirit in our midst.

PRESENTATION/ENTERTAINMENT TO PARTICIPATION/EXPERIENCE

Many books have been written about the move from presentation and entertainment worship to participation and experiential worship,[8] so I won't belabor this point. Suffice it to say that we need to focus on the ways in which worship is experienced, moving from a head to a heart knowledge of God. To invite participation in worship is to acknowledge that all the planning in the world won't allow for what might happen when individuals join in and change the outcome and the experience of worship. When we ask an artist to assist with the message, our part is, well, only *part* of the sermon. We won't always know how the service will turn out, but this is a reality of living in the mystery of a community of worship planners. Being willing to live in this mystery takes more risk, but

I believe it is more real. Worship is not for worship leaders alone but is a communal event. It's time we remember that again.

THE NEW-OLD REVIVAL

It is important to note that what is happening in worship these days is not as much "new" as it is "old." We have been quick to tout that we are doing a new thing in reaching out to the next generation, but what we are doing is in many ways going back to an ancient way of worship. For example, many who hold to a postmodern worldview love worshiping God in old sanctuaries rather than in boxlike auditoriums. They are fond of the mystery in old architecture and in stained glass and in sounds that bounce around high ceilings and marble posts. Recently I showed a young man our worship space. It was of the newer auditorium-style set for presentational worship. When we walked into the sanctuary, he had an immediate and visceral negative response, saying that he liked much better the old and beautiful spaces and that he could better sense God's presence in these places.

It's not just about the design of the space but about the move of culture to find value and meaning in the old traditions and ancient memories. The Apostles' Creed is a group of words that remind us of the connection we have with our parents, our grandparents, and Christ-seekers over time. This creed doesn't just teach us what we believe, but it connects us with all who believe and with Him in whom we believe.

The "new" change is to lean toward the old rather than the "modern." But really, it is more a change of mixing the old with the new so that today's people can hear and understand and know God.

ANSWERING THE STUCK-IN-THE-MUDS

If you've ever had the experience of being stuck in the mud, you know how hard it is to get out. You have to rock the car back and forth, and it helps to have someone push from behind. But the ones pushing get awfully dirty from the mud sprayed by the spinning tires. It's a heck of a mess to be in.

Sometimes our churches get in these kinds of places. Things are so familiar that we become comfortable, and we find ourselves in spots that are hard to get out of. Those who try to move things forward often get the dirtiest, if you know what I mean. We hear complaints and comments like, "Why change? I like it the old way." Or "We've always done it that way." You know the routine.

I am not an expert at answering the stuck-in-the-muds, but I have had my share of opportunities along these lines. What I can tell you is that people *do* understand that their children and grandchildren are missing out on the experience of God in their midst . . . and that it's been quite some time since many of their family members have graced the doors of a church. They are open and willing to learn how to reach those they love in their families.

Join in the conversation with them. Don't shy away from it! You might be surprised at how many stuck people become the creative thinkers of your congregation. After all, they know their grandkids!

SEEKING THE CREATOR

God, the Father, is often called "the Creator." God's essence is creativity. And because we are made in God's image, our essence is creativity too. Don't be afraid to find the creativity within you and within the people in the church. God delights in your imaginative and creative worship. It's not dull or boring or dead. It's active and deep and alive. Be creative, as God created you to be.

THE POTTER AND THE CLAY

Jeremiah 18:1–6

THE MESSAGE:

The sins/mistakes of your past are not set in concrete. Rather, they are in the hands of God, the Potter. God will remake, remold, and re-create you to be a vessel fit for service. Don't think that you are the Potter! Remember that you are the clay, and God alone can take your past and remold it to the perfect present and future.

THE BACKGROUND:

God has a message to speak to the people. In order to deliver the message to the prophet Jeremiah, God takes him down to the potter's house, where he can learn by watching the potter work. The message is a tough one: "You have sinned. Let Me remake you to the perfection I have in mind for you. Let Me be your Creator God, and trust your life to My hands." In order to be remade, God has to take the Israelites back to the center of who they are: a people who honor and worship only the one true God. The people did not want to hear this message (sound familiar?) and they rebelled. Their rebellion brought about their own demise. But the message is still crucial: God can make the foulest soul clean and fit for service!

THE CREATIVE AVENUE:

Roy Griffith is a potter who was a member of my second church, Mission Bell United Methodist. I was fascinated by the work he did in artsy Scottsdale, Arizona, and we began talking about it one day.

I told him my idea for this sermon, and he was immediately willing to give it a try.

During the sermon, Roy set up his potter's wheel at the center of the platform (using a drop cloth to cover the floor), and he began throwing a pot, working quietly while I talked. I told some stories:

1. The story of our church. How we had failed in many ways.

How God had begun a work of restoration in our midst.

2. The story of Jeremiah and the Israelite people. How they had rebelled and turned away from their Maker.

3. The story of my life. How I had failed to believe in God. How I had failed to trust in God after the death of my firstborn daughter.

4. Then I told of a God who could remake our mistakes, forgive our sins, and restore us to a vessel that could hold its water!

IMPORTANT NOTES:

In sequence two of the sermon, I began describing what Jeremiah sees at the potter's house: how the clay must be brought back to the center when a mistake is made. While I was discussing this, Roy intentionally threw a "mistake" into the pot, and it suddenly fell into an unformed lump on the wheel. Then he began to remake the pot again. When I got to this part of the sermon, there was an audible gasp as the lump of clay was thrown off kilter and became an unformed mass! Thanks to Roy, the point was made! You must do this sequence somewhere in the middle of the sermon if possible, so that you give the potter enough time to throw another pot.

The sermon was augmented also by Roy's facial gestures and body language as he visually responded to my sermon. Sometimes he would screw his face up in a frown, or raise his eyebrows in surprise, or silently chuckle in delight. Roy had the gift of multitasking, listening intently while he created an art form. And this gift spoke volumes as the people responded to his reactions.

EXTRAS:

- Throughout the chancel of the church, set out other clay pots the artist has created. Different-shaped pots make a statement all their own.
- For the children's moment, give the children a piece of clay for their hands to work while explaining how the potter represents God and the clay represents us.
- Pass out a lump of clay to every person as they leave the church (or as they enter).
- Place a picture of a potter on the front of the bulletin or on a screen.

ENDING:

To end this sermon, ask some musicians to sing "Change My Heart, O God." Then ask the congregation to sing along before ending with the benediction.

DAVID, DEPRESSION, AND THE HARP

Psalm 71:5–6, 17, 20–23

THE MESSAGE:

Depression hits everyone at some point in life. It takes on many forms such as discouragement, listlessness, lack of motivation, sadness, grief, or masked anger. One way or another, given a long life, we will face this emotion. We don't always want to talk about depression, seeing it as a state of failure, but if we can name it and recognize its power over our lives, then we can begin the healing process toward emotional wholeness.

This sermon begins by acknowledging that depression exists. Give examples of people you know who have gone through periods of depression. This is a good place to use a few well-chosen statistics about depression.

Then talk about these things:

1. King Saul's depression and how David played the harp to calm him.
2. David's depression as he faced his many enemies.
3. Your own experience(s) of depression.
4. What heaven might be like for you. (This is a counterpoint. For me, heaven would be lying in bed after a full day and hearing harp music as I fall asleep.) Here I told a story about Joyce, a fellow seminary student and harpist, carrying her harp to the Claremont School of Theology to play at chapel. She would practice the night before, as we were falling asleep, and it felt like we were in heaven. Joyce also plays for people

37

who are experiencing pain or stress, or who are dying. She has a wonderful ordained ministry that is enhanced by her harp playing.

5. Finding ways to overcome your moments of depression. Practical application.

THE BACKGROUND:

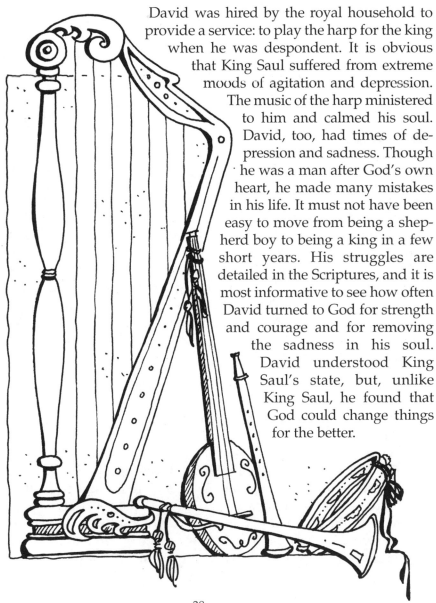

David was hired by the royal household to provide a service: to play the harp for the king when he was despondent. It is obvious that King Saul suffered from extreme moods of agitation and depression. The music of the harp ministered to him and calmed his soul. David, too, had times of depression and sadness. Though he was a man after God's own heart, he made many mistakes in his life. It must not have been easy to move from being a shepherd boy to being a king in a few short years. His struggles are detailed in the Scriptures, and it is most informative to see how often David turned to God for strength and courage and for removing the sadness in his soul. David understood King Saul's state, but, unlike King Saul, he found that God could change things for the better.

THE CREATIVE AVENUE:

Rev. Joyce Beukers played the harp with me during this sermon. We went back and forth and weaved the sermon together. Sometimes she played alone; sometimes she played as a background to my speaking; sometimes I spoke without any harp in the background. We weaved things together and back and forth. This took some practice. We went through the sermon the weekend before. But even so, every time we preached together, it was a new event. We listened for cues from each other and found weaving moments as they arose. You have to be willing to risk and trust with this one!

Because my sermons are in oral form (rather than a manuscript), I did not always stick to the outline. Sometimes I hit it, and many times I diverted! Still, it worked because Joyce was able to play off of my words and to fit in as she felt led by the music and the message.

IMPORTANT NOTES:

Be sure to give times in the sermon for harp music alone. Do not rush this time. The harp is relaxing and soothing, and will minister to the souls in your church. Center the harp and harpist on the platform. Preach from the sidelines. Practice the sermon beforehand so you have an idea about what the sound is like with the harp playing along with your voice. Do an audio check before the service to make sure both your voice and the harp can be heard.

EXTRAS:

Rev. Joyce Beukers also helped with the children's moment. She did a "show-and-tell" about the harp, which belonged to her beloved grandmother. She related music as a way to come into harmony with the Creator.

At the end of the service, the children came forward and Joyce let them touch the harp strings for themselves.

ENDING:

Give a benediction, and close with harp music. This will put people in a state of peace as they leave the sanctuary.

THREE SEEDS

HATS

Luke 10:38–42

THE MESSAGE:

This message was inspired by the song "Hats," from Amy Grant's *Heart in Motion* album (A&M Records, 1991). While jogging and listening to her music one day, I thought that the story of the "Hats" song would fit well into a sermon. We lead busy lives, wearing many hats and serving in many roles. Sometimes it seems we are literally running wild with things to do for every single role. I count each of my roles as wife, mother, daughter, sister, aunt, friend, and pastor as important. But how can I do everything I need to do in one day's time to satisfy all of my responsibilities in each of these roles? This message reminds us that there is really only one thing that is crucial: loving God. If we get that part right, the rest of our "hats" will fit properly into the space of our lives.

The message included these elements:

1. The many roles we play in our lives as described in the song "Hats."
2. I showed a photo of two of my children, Andrew and Natalie, as preschoolers, each wearing about ten hats piled up on top of their heads.
3. The sisters Mary and Martha learned about the one role that was most important: sitting at the feet of Jesus.
4. Sometimes it is easy to be in the presence of the ones we love, and sometimes it is difficult to be in the presence of the ones we love. (For example, when my husband was in school, I wanted to be near him all the time because he was forever busy

with his studies. On the other hand, when my son Andrew began wrestling, it was difficult for me to watch. I had to force myself to be there and to watch these young men throw one another around, including my son!)

5. Moses' veil covered his face because the people couldn't stand to see the glory of God. Jewish men wear yarmulkes to cover themselves out of respect for God. In the Catholic Church in Mexico, women wear scarves to cover their heads before God.

6. But Jesus changed that on the cross. The Temple veil was torn in two so that we could all be at the feet of Jesus.

7. During graduation from high school we set ourselves free from our past by tossing our caps into the air (see THE CREATIVE AVENUE; motion toward your hat). We are free to be focused on one thing: loving God. Toss hats!

THE BACKGROUND:

Jesus commends Mary to Martha, saying she understands the "one thing" that is crucial to life and that He won't take that away from her. Mary and Martha roles are typical in families. Usually there is at least one "do-er" and one "be-er" in each family. Jesus knew that Mary set aside the tasks that were required of her so that she could be at His feet to learn and to love her Teacher. In ancient times only men were allowed to "sit at the feet" of a master. Women were not permitted to be in this position of society, so Mary was doing something quite audacious for her time. Martha was doing the expected thing, and she was fuming because she wasn't getting any help with all that company. But Jesus calls us all to be focused on the "one thing" of loving God, despite the many hats we wear.

THE CREATIVE AVENUE:

I wanted people to experience wearing many hats in a short amount of time, mimicking our daily lives. So I gathered together hats from some of my friends and from the congregation. (Note: If you borrow hats, you can count on about ten hats per family. When you borrow from others, you will find that some remarkably funny hats will appear! Plus, this automatically makes the people participants in the shaping of the sermon.) Prior to the start of the service, I placed a hat underneath every chair in the worship center. Remember to place hats under the chairs of choir members, band leaders, and other worship leaders as well.

During the sermon, I asked the praise band leader to interrupt me about four times with music. I instructed the people that every time the music played, they were to get up and exchange hats with others in church (speaker and band included). Encourage them to go far from their seats to mix up the hats far and wide. Tell them they have to be back in their seats before the music ends. This adds urgency and speed to the moment, reminding them of the childhood game "Musical Chairs."

If you want, you can cue the musician when to interrupt you. I cued about four or five interruptions (musical hat switches) during the sermon. My cue was a hand signal behind my back, or you can do something like scratch your head. If you have a good working relationship, you might be able to trust the musician to interrupt whenever he or she wants, giving her a sermon outline ahead of time. This adds a natural feeling of truly being interrupted to the sermon giver!

At the end of the sermon, I spoke about graduation day and

described the experience of freeing ourselves from our hats and focusing on the "only thing" that matters: God. As I described the graduation event, I focused on the ritual of throwing hats into the air and while saying this, I took my hat off, encouraging everyone to follow me, and we flung our hats into the air. This cathartic moment freed us, and the response was applause, laughter, and the sounds of celebration in the worship center!

IMPORTANT NOTES:

- Remind folks who let you use hats to put their names in the hats. This is easy to do on a small piece of masking tape or with a permanent marker.
- On the following Sunday, set up the hats that haven't been collected on a table in the entry area. It makes for an easy collection and for a remembrance of a fun Sunday experience.
- Encourage the people to take hats to those who are in wheelchairs and to help out those who have trouble moving around.
- *Have fun with this one. Laughter makes it more memorable.*

EXTRAS:

Put a funny-looking hat on the altar. It will get people talking and wondering what's going on. People don't notice the hats under their chairs until you tell them about it, so the element of surprise usually remains until the end. Some observant people will ask about the hats under the chairs, and I gave them evasive, "wait and see" answers.

This is a great time for musicians to sing "Hats," by Amy Grant and Chris Eaton. Or you could play the song from the *Heart in Motion* CD and have a teen dance troupe perform it prior to the sermon.

ENDING:

After throwing the hats into the air, end with a prayer that focuses on the freedom from our many roles and on the "one thing" of loving God.

FOUR SEEDS

SHACKLES

Daniel 6

THE MESSAGE:

Daniel was faithful to God and to his king. The staff got jealous of Daniel's rise to power, and they set him up to end up in the lions' den. But Daniel remained true to his heart and ended up praising God because God freed him. God saves us from the lions' den in our lives.

The message includes these points:

1. Daniel in the lions' den
2. My own lions' den
3. The lessons from the den

THE BACKGROUND:

Daniel was just a boy when he was taken into captivity by the Babylonians. He was forced to leave his homeland of Judah and to enter into the town and culture of Babylon. There he was educated with the best, and he excelled in his studies. Daniel seemed to have it all. He was handsome, smart, wise, and a natural leader. The only thing Daniel lacked was freedom. His new culture demanded that he be Babylonian in all ways, changing his name to "Belteshazzar," training him in the Babylonian educational system, and even requiring that he worship their gods and their king.

While Daniel rose to the top of the heap because of his natural talents and abilities, he gained the respect of King Nebuchadnezzar. The king continued to put him in positions of leadership.

Daniel served him well and did all that he asked, except for one thing: he would not give up his God and worship the gods of the Babylonians. Although he had been stripped bare of all his beginnings and culture, Daniel refused to give up the God of his childhood. Daniel remained faithful. Daniel went on to serve well under three other kings: Cyrus, Cambyses, and Darius I.

THE CREATIVE AVENUE:

This sermon cropped up in my imagination because of the song "Shackles," from Mary Mary's *Thankful* album (Sony, 2000). The song describes being "shackled" by things that prohibit us from praising God. I asked the teens in my church to create a dance routine to this song and to perform it with me during the sermon. They created an original hip-hop version of dance. I had them dance to the song in the beginning of the sermon, setting them up beforehand. Then, at the end of the sermon, I joined the teens in the dance. While I am not a dancer by talent, they taught me a simplified version that I could handle. The dance at the end created surprise and invited all to join in the "dance" of praise to God our Creator.

I must admit that this sermon was done with much trepidation, mainly because I would be dancing in front of people. I felt like I was living out Wesley's admonition about preaching, "I set myself on fire, and they come to see me burn." I wondered if this sermon would burn out to a fizzle when I joined in the dance! It was a risky venture for me personally because I do not enjoy performance of any sort. However, I prayed that God would use it anyway, and somehow the message that we are all meant for praise, even during the hard times (see the words of the song "Shackles," by Mary Mary), would rise to the surface. It did. The creative moment at the end of the sermon was full of excitement and participatory praise to God.

Sometimes you risk looking foolish for God. I did in this instance. Remember—it's okay to laugh at yourself and at your inadequacies as you allow God to use you anyway!

EXTRAS:

During the dance, the boys made paper shackles to put around their hands and feet, and they broke the shackles to show the freedom of praise.

ENDING:

At the end of this sermon I invited everyone to stand and "dance" with me. Most stood and clapped and moved to the music. As the song ended, my hands were raised in praise and I invited the people to raise their hands as we said a prayer of praise to the God who sets our hearts free.

FIVE SEEDS

SHADOW

Psalm 91:1

*Those who live in the shelter of the Most High will find
rest in the shadow of the Almighty. (Ps. 91:1)*

THE MESSAGE:

When we choose to live in the shadow of the Almighty, we find
rest. Most often in our lives, we have no concept of the fact that
God is with us every moment. In this sermon, I hoped to provide a
powerful visual of God's presence, showing how that secure
knowledge can provide us with strength, comfort, and peace.

The message outline goes like this: band plays selections from
The Pink Panther, which could be dubbed over a video of Pink Panther segments. Choose clips where the Pink Panther is searching
for his shadow or like segments.

1. Describe shadows in our lives: the mirror is a shadow of our
   selves; the sun casts a shadow of our images; you can figure
   out the time of day by the position of the shadow from the
   nearby tree; when you don't get enough sleep, you have shadows under your eyes; if you forget to shave, you'll show the
   world the shadow on your face; and a shadow in the sky
   (clouds) produces rain.

2. The band plays and sings a medley of *The Pink Panther* theme
   song and "The Shadow of Your Smile" (written by Johnny
   Mandel and Paul F. Webster; recorded by Tony Bennett, by
   Frank Sinatra, and by Barbra Streisand).

3. Living in the Shadow of the Almighty. I wonder what it would look like or feel like if we really knew that the Shadow of the Almighty followed us everywhere? If I picture it, I see the Father, the Son, and the Holy Ghost all right behind me.

> *As I said this, three band members stepped out and stood behind me. I continued talking, and the three people shadowed me as I moved back and forth across stage. Move slowly so that your "shadowers" can keep up easily, but make definite movement back and forth. Have fun with this, even trying to out-step them once.*

4. Psalm 139, for example, might sound differently to us if we really knew that the Shadow was with us. *Read portions of Psalm 139.*

5. But there are times when we decide to leave the Shadow of the Almighty because we think that we can do life on our own.

> *Step away from the Shadow, the three people, motioning to them to stay where they are while you walk away alone.*

In the Bible, there are many descriptions of those who considered leaving or who actually did leave the Shadow of the Almighty:

- Moses left the Shadow of the Almighty when he despaired of his people who were complaining and moaning. And he said, "Oh, God, why don't You just kill me right here . . . I'd rather have death than have these people that You gave me!"
- Jonah went in a direction opposite of the way that God commanded.
- David chose another way even when he knew what God wanted him to do.
- Peter deserted his Lord and Savior.
- Saul of Tarsus knew the Book of the Law, but deserted the God who wrote the Book.

6. I had a time when I walked away from God's love. After the death of my first child, I stopped believing that there was a God. But God, in His mercy, drew me toward Him even as I was making mistakes. And there came a time when I FELL into the arms of God's love. (It is better to use your own story here if possible.)

As I began talking about my own experience, I slowly walked back toward the three people and when I said, "I fell," I literally fell into the arms of the Shadow. Prior to falling back, I flung my arms up over my head and fell backward into their arms. This is tricky and takes a little practice and trust in the three people. It helped me that the middle person was my husband, and he grabbed me under my arms while the other two hung on to my arms. As we practiced this, we got to where they caught me and let the "fall" take me almost to the ground before they lifted me up. This must be a moment of surprise, which means that you must practice and then trust! If you do it with good timing, you might hear a gasp from the congregation.

I fell, and God caught me. And when God caught me, then I turned myself around, and never again did I want to be out of the Shadow of God.

So I made a new choice: I would forever stay in the Shadow of the Almighty—the Father, the Son, and the Holy Spirit.

7. I follow God, choosing to remain in the Shadow.

   Now I position myself behind the Shadow, the three people, and as they walk back and forth across the stage, I follow them. They walk across the stage, and I follow so the audience can see us both.

8. The law of proximity says that you are relationally close to those you are closest to physically. For example, those who live physically closer to your dorm room will be relationally closer to you. In the barrio, we say, "Mi casa es su casa!" (My house is your house). We say that because we live close and therefore live together and are family.

9. So I choose to be in the Shadow of the Almighty.

   Here the three people, the Shadow, left me and went back to their instruments, and when I was finished they began playing "The Shadow of Your Smile."

THE BACKGROUND:

Shadows are an everyday phenomenon that we all know well. They are so much a part of our lives that we seldom take time to think about what they mean to us. In Psalm 91:1 God's shadow is described as a place of rest and a sure and present source of strength to those who choose to live within the Shadow.

Shadows are created when an object interrupts light rays or the source of light. Shadows are a hint of the object as it interplays with light. Have fun thinking of the many ways you use the word *shadow* in your everyday life.

In the Old Testament, powerful people are often said to provide the "shadow of protection" (Song of Sol. 2:3; Lam. 4:20; Ezek. 31:6). The Messiah is looked to as a shadow of things to come (Isa. 32:2; Ezek. 17:23), and throughout the Scriptures God is the final shadow of security (Ps. 36:7; Ps. 91:1; Ps. 121:5; Isa. 25:4; 49:2, and 51:16).

THE CREATIVE AVENUE:

The creative path for this sermon is twofold. That is because I started out with one creative avenue in mind (songs about shadows), and then another theme developed in the sermon preparation (God's presence) that called for a deeper layer of creativity. It is usually best to stick to one creative avenue, if for no reason other than ease of production. The harder the sermons are to create, the less likely we will use them as a tool. But this one developed with two creative forms, and it worked.

The first form was one of the most commonly used forms of creative sermons: music. Music is so complex and deep and varied that there are almost endless possibilities to weave music in with word and create a new feel to the sermon. For this one, I asked Cliff to put together a medley of culturally-based, familiar songs that had the word *shadow* in them. We began with *The Pink Panther* theme song (brings to mind shadows) and went into "The Shadow of Your Smile." The shadows medley was going to start and end the sermon.

Then I thought of being shadowed by the presence of God and asked the three members of the band to "shadow" me during a portion of the sermon and then return to their instruments for the final song. In the sermon preparation, we developed a place where I "fell" into the Shadow and the Shadow caught me. There was also a new decision when I decided to follow the Shadow (instead of the Shadow following me). In Wesleyan thought, the movement goes from prevenient grace (the Shadow follows me), to justifying grace (I leave the Shadow and then fall into the arms of the Shadow), to sanctifying grace (I follow the Shadow).

IMPORTANT NOTES:

Practice this one! Go over cues for transitions to song with the band leader, taking time to hear the medley and feel the musical message. Especially practice the fall. Continue practicing until you trust that you will be caught every time so that you can embellish the fall with confidence. Allow the band members time to practice walking behind and before you. Direct them to stay shoulder to shoulder. It may help to have the middle person put his or her arms around the outer two. Walk fairly slowly as you speak. Allow yourself to have some fun with this. Once when we did this sermon, the three people simultaneously put on Ray-Ban sunglasses behind me, without my prior knowledge. The audience began laughing, and I turned around to look at them and had a good laugh myself. The surprise and humor work with you.

EXTRAS:

We began this sermon with a *Pink Panther* video clip showing shadows. You can do this either as a start to the sermon or as a surprising start to the service.

ENDING:

A simple "Amen" after the ending song that is sung to God ("The Shadow of Your Smile") does well. Or, you can close with an invitational prayer:

> *God, I choose to follow You.*
> *I choose to be in Your presence.*
> *Stay beside me.*
> *Go before me.*
> *Catch me when I fall.*
> *And never, never let me go.*
> *And all God's people said . . . amen.*

SIX SEEDS

TICKTOCK

Acts 6:1–7

THE MESSAGE:

The theme of this message is that we have limited time in our lives and have to make choices about how to spend our time. Though a difficult problem for this day, this scripture passage encourages us to choose wisely.

1. Time as seen through the ages. Discuss how time has been measured through the ages (sun, moon, planets, and seasons). See http://physics.nist.gov/GenInt/Time/ancient.html for specific historical information.

2. The scripture story. Describe the decision that the church had to make regarding how to share their resources with the needy.

3. The problem. The apostles felt they were being tugged away from doing what they had been called to do (preach, teach, etc.), and they were wrestling with issues of how to use their time wisely.

4. Cliff Wright quote: "Time is the great equalizer." It is the only thing we share alike. We are all doled the same amount of time in a day.

5. Music. Music is based on time and rhythm (and sound). Music is about the rhythms of life.

6. Psalm 39:4: *"LORD, remind me how brief my time on earth will be. Remind me that my days are numbered, and that my life is fleeing away."*

7. The clock is ticking. Finish telling the scripture story, and remind the congregation that time is passing. Challenge them to use their time wisely, for the clock never stops.

THE BACKGROUND:

The early church was growing exponentially. This "perfect" church was adding members by the thousands, but there were some "rumblings" going on as they rapidly increased. It seems that as they cared for one another by sharing their food, some inequalities became apparent. A hint of racial discrimination was the charge: the Greeks were complaining that the Hebrews were getting more resources and that the Greek widows were not getting enough food.

So they did what all good churches knew to do: they called a meeting. And as the apostles and church leaders wrestled back and forth about what was going on, they came to a place where they began to look at another issue—not the issue of equitable distribution of resources, but the issue of how they (the apostles) were spending their time arguing about this issue. They began to ask the question of themselves, "Should we really be spending our time running a food program, or should we be preaching the Word?"

For example, much of my day is spent in administration and planning for this church. And some of it is very necessary. But there are days when I think, "Shouldn't I be about the business of my calling?" Shouldn't I be praying, studying, preaching, and writing? Why am I trying to figure out the business of the church when there are people who could do that part of it so much better than me?

THE CREATIVE AVENUE:

The sound of a ticktock will be the backdrop for this service. You can use it in various ways. You could:

1. Start and end the service with the sound of a clock.
2. Use the ticktock sound in between sequences of the message.
3. Start out each song with a ticktock sound.

Find the ticktock sound on the Internet or on another resource, and amplify the sound through your sound system. This takes some work on timing with your tech team. Be sure they are confident of when to come in with the sound. If a mistake is made, just play along with it. It will only add to the feel of time ticking on.

IMPORTANT NOTES:

Give the tech team or sound person a written outline of when you want the sound to interrupt the service or sermon.

Have the tech team or sound person practice this one beforehand. They must feel very confident of the sound and of their permission to "interrupt" the message or service.

This one is simple! It adds such depth with just an extra sound. Be sure to listen to the tech team to see if they have any ideas about how to improve the service. This is their area of expertise, so listen to their advice!

EXTRAS:

- Refer to watches. Ask how many people in the congregation are wearing watches, and have them lift their watches up high.
- Ask how many people check the time of day on their cell phones, and ask them to raise their cell phones to show their timepieces.
- Ask how many people do not use any timepiece during the day (show of hands).

ENDING:

My favorite way to end this service is to say the benediction and then hear the "ticktock" sound overhead as people leave the sanctuary.

SEVEN SEEDS

INTERRUPTIONS

Mark 5:21–43

THE MESSAGE:

Life is full of interruptions. Sometimes it seems not a day goes by without major interruptions to our plans. We may start out each and every day with a plan, but invariably, the plans of mice and women are changed by unexpected and unplanned-for events.

Once I was interrupted while preaching a sermon. A little three-year-old girl jumped out of her chair and shouted to me, "Dottie, I've got to go potty!" Her interruption even rhymed! Of course, everyone laughed as I pointed her to the bathroom, and her mother rushed out to help her. You never know when life will throw you an interruption.

Some common interruptions in life:

1. Money. "I have to make ends meet and can't live on less."
2. Age. "I'm too old for that!"
3. People's expectations. "I have to be the mom, husband, boss, and assistant."
4. Grief. "I lost a dream already. Can't lose another one."
5. Failure. "I can't risk failing. So, I just won't try."

What is your excuse?

Tell the story of Jairus's daughter, which, you see, is a story of a major interruption. Tell this story at length with as much attention to detail as possible. See THE BACKGROUND for planned interruptions.

The good news is that life doesn't have to be perfect before good things happen. Even in the midst of your interrupted life, Jesus can bring healing, wholeness, and great joy. Your dream may have been interrupted. You may not have become the person you knew you were meant to be. You may not have followed your call, or even listened to your call. But it's not too late! It's never too late! Even an interrupted life can be beautiful and full and filled with God's grace.

THE BACKGROUND:

Jairus was a well-respected man in his community. He held the coveted position of leader of the local synagogue. His position was similar to the position of president of the board of directors or chair of the administrative council in your church. When Jairus spoke, everyone would listen! But Jairus had a problem: his daughter, his beloved little cherub-faced daughter, was sick—"nigh unto death," as they say—and Jairus was desperate.

So he sought out Jesus, the Healer. Now mind you, Jesus was not recommended by the Temple leaders. They viewed Him as a radical man who was saying some bizarre things like, "I am the Son of God," and "No man comes to the Father except through Me." Weird stuff! But Jairus was desperate for love of his baby, and so he sought out the only One he knew who had healed anyone: Jesus.

✴ (Now tell of a time when someone you loved was sick and you were desperate for a touch of healing from God.)

Jairus was feeling desperate, so he went to Jesus. Truly Jairus is a man to be envied because he did what we all wish we could do. He told his problem to Jesus, and Jesus went with him. He had Jesus go where he wanted Him to go. What we wouldn't give to have a moment of knowing that we had Jesus going our way!

So Jesus was going where Jairus wanted Him to go when He was so rudely INTERRUPTED!

INTERRUPTION...

(Now continue the story...) A woman had been hemorrhaging for years, twelve to be exact, when she too saw Jesus in the crowd. She reached out and touched Him in desperation because no matter what anyone else thought, she would do anything to be healed.

She had tried all the remedies. In those days, some of the "cures" for hemorrhaging were:
- Tonics
- Carrying the ashes of an ostrich egg in your pocket

- Carrying around a barley corn that had been found in the dung of a white she-ass[9]

There were more, but you get the picture. She had tried everything. She had spent all her money on doctors and quacks and anyone who might have a cure. She knew she wasn't supposed to be in the crowd where her disease might make someone else unclean, but she didn't care on that day. She just wanted to be healed, so she reached out and touched the hem of Jesus' robe and, instantly, she was cured.

Jesus stopped. Having felt the power leave Him, He asked, "Who touched Me?" This was a silly question given the fact that He was surrounded by a crowd of people pressing in on Him from all sides. But this was different; Jesus knew that He had released healing to someone. The woman, scared spitless, said, "I did." Jesus reassured her that she had been healed and sent her on her way.

INTERRUPTION...

Meanwhile, Jairus was more than a little bit perturbed. Desperation had turned to all-out grief because while Jesus was being interrupted, messengers came to him to say, "Your little girl is dead. Don't bother Jesus anymore."

But Jesus asked Jairus to trust Him. Even in the interruption of life.

They arrived. Were they silent? What must Jairus have thought on the way to his house? Was he wondering if Jesus would have saved his daughter if He had not stopped to help that bleeding woman? Did he feel guilty for even thinking that?

His stomach must have jumped into his throat when he saw his yard. The mourners were carrying on in true customary fashion, making it obvious that she was dead. The crowd laughed at Jesus when He told them, "She is only asleep." He parted the crowd and went in.

Jesus took her hand in His and said, "Get up, little girl!" And the dear little twelve-year-old daddy's girl immediately stood up and walked around! Jesus told them to feed her, which I'm sure they did with gusto!

THE CREATIVE AVENUE:

Form your sermon as you normally would, and write INTERRUPTIONS into your message. Ask some volunteers to help you with this, and assign them different places in the message to interrupt you. When I did this, the people I asked to help threw in an extra interruption that I hadn't planned on, and they really surprised me! It added to the feel of life's stopping places.

Some interruptions might be:

1. Someone walks across the front with a big sign that says, "APPLAUSE!" Hopefully the congregation will start clapping.
2. Someone jumps in and asks for everyone with February (whatever month it is) birthdays to stand up and lead in singing "Happy Birthday to You!"
3. Another person jumps in and asks everyone to move over one seat to the right.
4. Someone forcefully hits a gong or a cymbal during the message, creating a startling sound.

IMPORTANT NOTES:

You will likely have to choose outgoing personalities to interrupt you, and you will have to coach them. Encourage them to be demonstrative in their interruptions. Ask them to play this up and allow humor to come through their actions. Tell them they are helping to create a setting where the true meaning of the scripture comes alive.

The element of surprise is the work of art in this one! You don't have to prepare the congregation at all. They will get it soon enough, although they might be extremely uncomfortable during the first interruption. They will understand when you start describing interruptions in life and in the Word. Have fun!

The idea for this sermon came while listening to the Rev. Dr. E. V. Hill preach on this passage. He must be wowing the angels with his expositions even now!

EXTRAS:

1. Be sure that the "APPLAUSE!" sign is big enough for the back row to read.
2. Make sure your volunteers are miked and can be well heard.
3. Practice this with your volunteers beforehand until they are comfortable with your cues.

ENDING:

Say, "God bless you. God bless your interruptions!"

EIGHT SEEDS

WHEN GOD CRIED

2 Corinthians 4:8–12, 16–18

THE MESSAGE:

This sermon was formed on the one-year anniversary of September 11, 2001. The message parts are:

1. Describe a recent storm. I've always thought that the rain was like God's big alligator teardrops on the earth, watering our land through the pains of life. On this particular eve of the September 11 anniversary, it rained in our city. I thought, "How appropriate! God is crying for the memory of the pain and loss."

2. Things that make God cry. I think there are times God really has a good old cry. For example:

   a. When the Israelites were involved in human sacrifice to other gods, and they sent their children to their deaths
   b. When the religious leaders of the day nailed His Son to the cross
   c. When the tragedy of September 11 hit our skies

3. Rev. David Benke. I read about this Missouri Synod Lutheran pastor who was suspended from his denomination because he joined hands with religious leaders of other denominations and faiths to pray for the victims of September 11 at the memorial service at Yankee Stadium. He was labeled a "syncretist" by his tribe. God must have cried.

4. Describe other stories of your memories of September 11.

Most of the heartfelt stories I found in the book *What We Saw*, by CBS news.

5. Address Scripture's message to those who are hurting. Bring out the hope that is present even in the midst of great tragedy.

THE BACKGROUND:

This message was timely for a particular moment in history (the events of September 11, 2001), but there will be other times in history in which sadness pervades our nation or our world, and for these moments, this message is crucial.

The Scripture says that we share in the death of Jesus and that even our bodies share in that event. We respond to life in the present, but we are also a part of what happened to our Lord in the past. We carry the scars of living, and our souls are damaged by evil. But even in the face of death, eternal life and eternal hope will rise. This happens because Jesus paid the price for our love and because He already feels our moments of pain. The hope is in eternity and in the experience of hope that good wins out over evil.

Therefore, we can express the pains of life knowing that Jesus felt them too. And we can look at that pain head-on, knowing that He has already overcome whatever we face.

THE CREATIVE AVENUE:

I went to a local arts-and-crafts store and bought blue crystal stones to represent the tears that God cried on September 11. I bought one "tear" for each life that was lost on that day, and I put them in a crystal bowl on the altar.

After the message, I asked the congregation to come to the altar and grab a handful of "tears." I asked them to keep one "tear" as a reminder of the moments when God cries and to pass out the others to friends, explaining what the stones represent.

I was surprised that all of the "tears" were gone before the service was over. People grabbed huge handfuls—even pocketfuls—and seemed excited to have their share.

Throughout the week following this sermon, I heard stories from people who passed out the "tears of God." The little blue stones proved to be a powerful tool for people to share God's love in their communities of work, friends, and family.

EXTRAS:

You may also want to use water as an additional symbol of God's tears. For example, place on the altar a bowl filled with water. Especially powerful is a bowl filled with rainwater that has been collected from a recent storm.

This could be a good time to do a Remembrance of Baptism ritual, reminding people of the death and resurrection of Jesus.

ENDING:

Encourage people to share their tears and their stories with one another this week. Ask them to remember where they were and what they were doing when they heard about the tragedy of September 11. Encourage them to remember where they could see glimpses of hope.

BAGGAGE

1 Samuel 10:17–24

And the LORD replied, "He is hiding among the baggage." (1 Sam. 10:22)

THE MESSAGE:

The theme of this message is, "Don't hide out among your life's baggage!" God sees you even when you are hiding, so get out of your hiding place and follow the call on your life to seek and to save the lost.

1. Describe a baggage car (I described one I saw on a train, but you may want to focus on the baggage department at the airport, or another example). Especially describe the mess that exists (the disorder) among the baggage.

2. The scripture story: Israel wanted a king and Samuel was following God's directive to find one. Tell the story of how Samuel found Saul, especially how Saul was hiding out among the baggage instead of stepping up to his place of honor.

3. Hiding out among your baggage. Sometimes our "baggage" prevents us from accomplishing our life's mission. We have many excuses for not living out our purpose in life, much as King Saul did. The simple fact is that we have been created to take God's Good News and God's love to our world. What is the baggage that you are hiding behind?

4. Tell the mission of your church, and describe how each person connects into the greater mission of the church in the world.

5. The end of the scripture story: Saul's life as a king was not what it could have been. He continued to make excuses for his position. He was mad at David for his popularity. He fought the evils of jealousy, control, and distrust. He fought the demons of anxiety and stress. In the end, Saul lost out on what could have been his because of the ways he hid among his own baggage.

6. Speak to the people about their issues with baggage. Tell a story of someone who has overcome many challenges to focus on their true purpose in life.

THE BACKGROUND:

Israel was first ruled by judges like Samuel and his sons. But Samuel's sons were corrupt judges who accepted bribes and manipulated justice. So when Samuel was an old man, the people begged for a king who could rule them like other nations were ruled. (The grass sure looked greener on the other side!) A king, Samuel warned, could be very harsh. After all, a king could draft their sons into a war, bring about slave labor for the kingdom, use their daughters for the palace, and bring on taxation! Samuel warned the people, but they didn't care. They still wanted a king. In their minds, anyone would be better than Samuel's sons!

So Samuel agreed to look for the king that the Lord had in mind for them. He found Kish, a rich and influential man from the tribe of Benjamin, who had a handsome son named Saul. Saul was tall and had the appearance of a king, and Samuel anointed him after one look. The Lord had chosen a king.

THE CREATIVE AVENUE:

This one is easy to execute. Simply create a visual backdrop by piling suitcases, backpacks, and shoulder bags next to your preaching space. You can also add purses and fanny packs for effect. The idea is to have a mountain of baggage that you stand beside (sometimes move in front of) as you preach.

The visual need not be explained or pointed out. It will speak for itself.

Choose a class or group in your church to make the mountain of luggage. Let them pile up the suitcases in a disorderly but high heap.

EXTRAS:

If there is someone in your congregation who knows how to shoot and edit video, ask them to create a video collage of baggage piles from the airport, hotels, bus stations, and closets. You can also create this with still photographs put together into a slide show. Find a traveling song to put underneath the video or slide show. You can then project the images onto a screen during the service.

ENDING:

Challenge the people to go forth into the world, baggage or no baggage. Remind them not to hide, but to put behind the past and the excuses and to go forward with the One who makes all things right and beautiful!

TEN SEEDS

BEAUTIFUL FEET!

Romans 10:11–15; Exodus 3

THE MESSAGE:

Talk about feet! They seem to be unimportant and perhaps even ugly, but the book of Romans tells us that feet are beautiful. Look at feet in the Bible, and connect feet to telling the Good News.

1. High school assignment: I had to write a poem about the ugliest part of my body. I described my feet: the corns, the calluses, the crooked toes, and the dry places.

2. Examples of feet in the Bible:
   a. Woman anoints Jesus's feet with expensive oil (John 12:1–11).
   b. Jesus washes the disciples' feet at the Passover meal and tells us to go and do the same (John 13:13–14).
   c. Disciples see Jesus after the Resurrection, and they take hold of His feet and worship Him (Matt. 28:9).

3. Story of Moses at the burning bush. Tell how Moses was asked to take off his shoes as a sign of the holiness of his call (Exod. 3:1–15).

4. Scripture in Romans. Speak about the Romans text and about the beauty of those who bring the Good News. Remind the congregation that this is not referring only to pastors but to anyone who brings the Good News to the hopeless and helpless in our society. Give an example of a way that this has happened recently in your church.

5. Encourage the people with beautiful (if stinky!) feet to be about the business of bringing the Good News. And brag over the beauty of their feet!

THE BACKGROUND:

Frederick Buechner, an acclaimed writer, wrote this in his book *Wishful Thinking* (HarperSanFrancisco, 1993):

> *Generally speaking, if you want to know who you really are,*
> *as distinct from whom you like to think you are,*
> *keep an eye on where your feet take you.*[10]

In Bible times, people traveled by foot, leaving feet tired and dirty. It was a hospitality custom to wash the feet of a guest. Often this duty was performed by the lowliest of servants. Another custom, anointing someone's feet, was done to those who received high honor.

The Israelites in the Old Testament came up with the idea of "beautiful are the feet." This phrase explained the times when a messenger would bring good news to the field of battle. They were awaiting news that the battle was being waged well, that their loved ones were still alive, and that the fight was still on. Whatever the news, as we know, it is always better to know the news than to not know, even when the knowing brings much pain. To be a foot-traveling messenger was a position of value![11]

In Greek, the word for "gospel" means "good news." For the Hebrews, *bisar* is about the good announcement given in a battle. For Christians, the "Good News" is that Jesus has risen, conquering sin and death! With that assurance, we can look at those who proclaim these messages of hope and say, "What beautiful feet they have!"

THE CREATIVE AVENUE:

At the beginning of the message, ask everyone who is able to take off their shoes and place them on the area around the altar, or somewhere in the front of the sanctuary. Have musicians play some background music while people take off their shoes and move to put them near the altar.

You can comment about the types of shoes you see. Are there many working shoes, tennis shoes, or high-heels? Are they fancy, plain, colorful, or simple? How do they smell as a group? Ha!

The visual of shoes is a constant reminder, and it peaks the interest of the people, causing them to wonder why you had them remove their shoes. It also brings people right into the message because they have contributed to your words.

EXTRAS:

For a children's moment, bring in your children's favorite baby shoes. Describe how each shoe fit the personality of that child. Then tell them about the scripture that describes beautiful feet. Describe the beauty of their feet, how they function to hold up the body and to provide balance. Give their feet a special blessing.

ENDING:

Bless their beautiful feet. After this blessing, have people come back to the front and put on their shoes.

ELEVEN SEEDS

THE WEDDING

John 2:1–11

THE MESSAGE:

Jesus began His ministry, His life's work, at a wedding. They say, "Actions speak louder than words," and by this action, Jesus was saying that families are important!

1. Describe Cana: The name Cana means "nest." This reminds us of "nesting." Before a baby is born, a mom and dad experience the "nesting instinct" and wildly clean the house, do last-minute shopping, cook, and generally spend crazed moments of time in preparation for the big event.

2. Tell the story of the wedding at Cana. Intersperse this story with a wedding story of your own. I'm sure you've got a funny one!

3. Actions speak louder than words. Once when I went to a wedding, the groom placed a flower on an empty chair where his mom would've sat if she were still alive. By doing so, he let us know that his mom's presence at this event was important, and that in some eternal-perspective kind of way, she was truly with him. Nothing was said to point out the flower or the empty chair, but since we all loved him and knew him, we knew that Ben was honoring his beloved mother on this important day in his life.

4. Renewal of wedding vows (see THE CREATIVE AVENUE).

5. Renewal of family vows. Lead the congregation in a pledge to honor the love of family. Have them repeat after you a pledge you write that includes words of forgiveness, faithfulness, and covenant to bring out the best in one another. Have the congregation stand during this vow.

THE BACKGROUND:

The Gospel of John has a wonderful format. If you look closely, there is a simple story that is told, and then behind that story, if you choose to look, there is a deeper meaning that is full of wisdom and provides gems of truth.

This story is like that. On the surface, it's a story about a wedding that Jesus and His mother and disciples attended. A simple family wedding with typical family problems. These always come out at weddings (trust me; I've been to many of them!). At one wedding I officiated, I went in to see if the bride was ready, and she was in tears after having witnessed a screaming match between her mother and her maid of honor. Weddings are so very interesting! At the wedding at Cana, the family problem was that the wedding planner hadn't planned too well. The interesting thing about this wedding is that many think the planner was Mary, the mother of Jesus. Because of the way the story is laid out, it is very possible that Mary was in charge of this wedding (she orders the servants around, indicating her responsible position). It is recorded in the Coptic Gospels that Mary was the sister of the groom's mother, or in other words, she was the aunt. Some nonbiblical writings about this event say that the groom was John himself (the writer of this Gospel and one of the disciples). We don't know this for sure, but we can make a good guess.

According to Jewish law, a virgin's wedding would be celebrated on a Wednesday. It is possible, given the order of events, that this wedding actually took place the week after the Sabbath on which Jesus met and called His disciples Andrew and John. This may have been why they stayed with Him for the week of celebrations.

Back in the day, these weddings were *the* happening events of the village. Typically, ceremonies would take place in the evening, after which the bride and groom were paraded through the town with a canopy over their heads and flaming torches to light the way. There was no escaping the family and friends for a honeymoon. Instead, the couple remained at their home for a full week, holding an "open-door policy" for any and all visitors. They were treated like the king and queen, complete with a total makeover and people who met their every need for pampering. It was a week of village participation in full-out care for the wedded couple.

In this particular week of festivities for the couple and the village, the hosts ran out of wine. And we know the rabbinic saying was, "Without wine, there is no joy." They weren't drunkards, for that was condemned by their laws, but they connected wine with the hospitality code of welcoming. So running out of wine signified an unwelcoming or uncaring gesture by the hosts. In Jesus' day, hospitality was on par with godliness (not cleanliness, as we like to think today!), and not to be a good host or hostess was the ultimate insult, especially at an event in which you were given plenty of time to prepare. It would be like inviting a bunch of teens over to the house and running out of Coke and potato chips. "Mom, we're starving! Why didn't you go to the store?" Oh, the horror of inhospitality! So the family was red-faced—no wine at a wedding, for goodness' sake![12]

Mama sees the dilemma. How could they run out of wine and face the village in the morning? And so she did what all good mothers do. She pushed Jesus into the adulthood stage of His calling, pushing Him out of His nest and into His ministry. She set Jesus free from the obligations that might have fallen to Him as the eldest child in a fatherless family (Joseph, according to tradition, died early) so that He could live out His life's calling. It's as if Mary were saying, "I'm okay, son. Now go and do YOUR job on earth . . . and oh, by the way, You can start by revealing Yourself when You change this water into wine!"

THE CREATIVE AVENUE:

The renewal of wedding vows is a short ceremony that is powerful in its effect. In the middle of this sermon, have a couple from your church stand up and renew their vows in front of the congregation. When we did this, the couple dressed up in a tuxedo and a wedding gown. You can even gather their family and friends around them to act as witnesses to their vows. Complete this scene with bits and pieces of the wedding march.

EXTRAS:

You could have some fun by having the couple end the service with a waltz.

ENDING:

At the end of the message, invite the congregation to stand, and lead them in a renewal of family vows together.

TWELVE SEEDS

LETTING GO!
The Exodus

Exodus 6:10–13

THE MESSAGE:

1. Tell the story of Moses' life including his birth and adoption, his flight into the desert, the call at the burning bush, and finally the call to return to Egypt and free his people. This story should be told in full and could take up most of the message.

2. Discuss the things that keep us in captivity in our lives, and then explain God's redemptive plan to set us free.

3. Tell of a time when God set you free.

4. Set the balloons free (see THE CREATIVE AVENUE).

5. Pray for hearts set free and for the grace to let go!

THE BACKGROUND:

Moses was chosen by God to speak to Pharaoh and specifically to bring about the release of his people from slavery. Moses grew as a leader and had to teach himself how to be "set free" from his own inadequacies, failings, and relationships. God convinced Moses that since He made Moses' mouth, He could probably help him with his words. And then God gave Moses a backup plan in the form of his family, Aaron and Miriam.

Moses heard the complaints all along the way. He knew that the people were settled in their slavery and that his interference in their lives was only making things harder on them. He heard them cry out for him to stop, and yet God kept instructing him to go on.

It's not always easy to be set free. Being set free means having to learn a new way of living. Being set free means having to trust what is not known. Being set free means having to lean on God instead of on our own competencies.

And, it's not easy to let ourselves go either. To be given freedom is only the first step. The next important step is to live in freedom. The people complained that things weren't so bad back in Egypt. They had good food, a roof over their heads, and regular working hours. They had to learn how to trust God for their food, how to follow the cloud by day and fire by night for their covering, and how to work twenty-four hours a day, six days a week. It was a different rhythm. A new tune. A whole new way of life.

But that is what God calls us to do: to be free and to let go. To live new every day. The challenge of letting go is just that: a challenge.

THE CREATIVE AVENUE:

Each person should be given a helium balloon when they enter the service. The balloons can be multicolored, or you can pick a theme color like blue or purple (to represent pain). Ask parents to help kiddos hold on to the balloons so they don't fly away in the middle of the service. Be prepared, however, for one balloon (or more!) to float to the ceiling and to pop loudly if it touches a hot light. Be ready for a quick one-liner to recover from such an event, and go ahead and laugh about it!

At the end of the message, ask people to think of either something they need to let go of or something God has freed them from. After you have given some time so that people's thoughts are firmly in their heads, then tell them to release the balloons into the air all at the same time. Watch the balloons rise, and when they reach the ceiling, have people hold hands and pray a prayer of release together.

The balloons will fall down to the ground in time, but you'll have them up there for a day or two, so beware of planning something special in the space the next day.

EXTRAS:

For the children's moment, talk about how hard it is to let go of something special. Remind them of letting go of a special blanket or a pacifier, and then talk about what it would be like if you went to school with a pacifier or a raggedy blanket in tow. Ask them to watch for the chance to "let go" of something during this service.

ENDING:

Use a song to put a period on this one. Choose a song that speaks of freedom or of Moses' cry to "let my people go!" Preferably pick a song that everyone can sing along to.

GRACE: BREAKING THROUGH THE BARRIERS

John 20:19–23

THE MESSAGE:

1. Nonorganic-failure-to-thrive babies. This inability to thrive in infants can sometimes be due to being left in cribs alone and without regular touch. When infants are neglected in this way, they can literally die. Not being touched is the worst curse of all.

2. Lepers in ancient days: the untouchables.

3. Living without touch. My dentist once said to me, "Touch is the only sense we can't live without." Helen Keller lived without two senses, and yet she relied on touch to communicate by signing out words on others' hands. The touch cells cover the whole body. Without touch, we wouldn't know when we were being burned, when we were loved, when it was cold, or when we had a fever. With touch, we feel the wind on our faces, the tears on our cheeks, the softness of a baby's skin, and the warmth of a blanket. Without touch, we would be clueless to the wonders of the world.

4. Jesus heals the leper, one who society said was unworthy to worship God (attend public worship). Jesus broke through boundaries with a hint of anger and an immediate response.

5. Describe untouchables today (e.g., homosexuals, undocumented residents, poor folks, etc.).

6. Describe someone you have treated as an "untouchable."

7. End the message with a "movement to break barriers" (see THE CREATIVE AVENUE). This story should be one about going out of the way to break barriers. Begin this sequence by describing the barrier created by preaching from a platform (separation of priest and people), and then move into your other chosen story. I told about Norman Vincent Peale, who told of an African missionary-teacher who received a beautiful seashell as a gift from one of his students. The boy had gone on foot to a faraway section of the African coast to get the shell. The missionary said to the boy, "You've gone so far to bring me such a wonderful gift!" The boy replied, "O teacher, long walk part of gift." It may be a long walk for us to go where we don't want to go, to go to the places unknown, to bridge our biases and prejudices, and to take God's love to the untouchables of our day, but,

---

I want to be like Jesus, and
long walk part of gift![13]

THE BACKGROUND:

Leprosy in Jesus' day was a societal problem. Lepers were covered with running sores and suffered through their day with a disease that was outwardly evident. Leprosy would eat away the skin, often resulting in the loss of fingers and toes. If you saw a leper, you had to yell, "Unclean!" and get as far away as possible from that person. For the Hebrews, a person who had leprosy was also deemed ceremonially unclean, which means they were unfit to worship God. Lepers, then, were isolated from the community in every possible way, including from the community of worshipers.

Jesus did not value the outward condition and certainly did not hesitate to touch, pray for, and heal the leper. In Mark 7:7, Jesus explains that the heart, not the outward appearance, is what matters when it comes to worship. When Jesus heals the leper, He heals one whom society categorizes as "unworthy" to worship.

THE CREATIVE AVENUE:

During the last sequence of the sermon, move from the pulpit area into the middle of the congregation, touching people on the shoulder as you move into their midst. To prepare for this, take out a few chairs in the middle to make a small aisle in the center of the church. If you have a large sanctuary, put a small riser in the middle, and you will end up telling your last story on that riser, in the midst of the people.

In essence, you are "breaking the barrier" between priest and people by leaving your pulpit and becoming one with them.

EXTRAS:

This would be a good Sunday to hire a mime artist and have him or her open the service by miming barriers, climbing over walls, etc.

ENDING:

Give the benediction from the center of the congregation, dismissing them to touch the "untouchables" and to break through barriers to love all of God's people.

FOURTEEN SEEDS

SENT!

Luke 24:35–49

THE MESSAGE:

1. The Scripture says to deliver the message and know that God is the One who brings the fruit. Our job is to tell the story. God's job is to produce fruit. Explain that we are sent to tell! Then discuss the root of the word *martyr*, which means "witness" and "to face in the right direction."

2. Has your church "arrived" or is your church "sent"?

3. Missionaries who are commissioned by The United Methodist Church are given an anchor cross as a reminder of their calling. This symbol consists of a cross that is in the center of an anchor, paying tribute to the fact that many missionaries have traveled by sea to arrive in the land to which they have been sent. As Christians, we have a rich missionary tradition.

4. Describe your neighborhood in depth. Tell about what you see: signs of poverty, loneliness, youth, elderly, disrepair, etc.

5. Culture wants church and needs the message of Christ. Did you notice how America went to TV-church when President Reagan died in June 2004? America attended a weeklong tribute and worship service together. Our culture is crying out for God!

6. *Send* means "to propel," or "to cause to go."[14] Are we "sent" Christians? Are we out there in the world, taking the gospel to the streets of our lives?

7. Tell a personal story of someone who is asking life questions. For example, my husband, Jim, is an optometrist, and one day a young woman named Darcy came in to have her eyes checked. After the examination, Jim asked Darcy if she had any questions for him. Darcy promptly replied, "Yeah. Will I find my true love?" The questions are there. Deep questions meant to be answered. People are seeking help with their lives. Are you listening to the questions of those to whom you have been sent?

THE BACKGROUND:

If you were told that you have only a limited time on this earth, you would choose your last words carefully. For this reason alone, we can see that the last words of Jesus to His disciples in Luke are words that we must listen to with great attention. Jesus said that they (and we) must take the message of repentance to everyone, that they must be the witnesses, and that they had a story to tell the world. Most of what Jesus said to them was about speaking out the Good News to God's world.

In the church we have a rich history of missionaries. We typically think of missionaries as those who are sent to far-off lands. But today's mission fields are not only across the seas but also in our neighborhoods. We are quickly becoming a nation that does not know the story of Jesus. If we won't tell them, who will?

THE CREATIVE AVENUE:

After the first sequence, tell the people that you need their help with this message. Explain that during the rest of the sermon, you will be walking around and touching people on the shoulder. When they have been touched, they should stand up and move out to form a circle around the edge of the sanctuary. If you have a large congregation, you can have each person touch someone else near them as they leave. As you are talking, they will be forming a circle around the edges. If at the end of your message you still have people sitting, ask those in the circle to go and touch someone to bring them out. Be sure to explain to those who have difficulty moving about that it is okay for them to remain seated!

As you end your message, ask everyone to sing along to an easy-to-follow song that focuses on being sent.

Then ask everyone to face outward and give the benediction to them in the sent-out-to-the-world position.

EXTRAS:

Prepare for the ending song with your worship leader. Make this a familiar and easy song.

ENDING:

The congregation is already in the position to leave, so wish them farewell with God's blessings!

FIFTEEN SEEDS

SEEDS IN FERTILE GROUND

Matthew 13

THE MESSAGE:

The theme of this message is to show how a small seed nurtured with proper care can produce great growth. We need God's grace and the community of believers for guidance and discipleship.

1. Scripture story. Explain some basic botany. Talk about how plants grow in various environments.

2. Show a video of children planting and caring for plants (see THE CREATIVE AVENUE).

3. Tell a story for each of these examples:
   a. A new Christian who does not receive discipleship from a Christian community and quickly falls away from his or her faith
   b. A Christian who falls away from faith under temptation
   c. A Christian with good intentions who is caught up in the cares of society and lets faith get crowded out by worldly concerns
   d. A Christian who surrounds himself or herself with a community of faith, takes the time for discipleship and nurturing of faith, and gradually produces fruit

4. The promise of a seed. A seed is a small thing that brings about much promise with proper care.

THE BACKGROUND:

The term seed" comes from the word *sperma*, which means "to sow." "To sow" means "to put in the ground" so that nature can do its work.[15] As Christians we seem to think that we are called to make sure we are bearing fruit, emphasis on *bearing*. That is hard work and is really an impossible job for a human to do. Farmers plant (sow) seed and care for the seed, but it grows because of nature's way. So do people. As Christians we can plant and care for seed, but it is God who makes fruit grow. We have a *part* in the process, but we are not *the* process.

In this passage, Jesus focuses on the soil, on the places where we plant seed. We cannot always plant in good soil, but we keep seeding, sowing, planting, and caring, knowing that God will concentrate on the growing.

THE CREATIVE AVENUE:

Set the altar table with four plants. Plant a fast-growing seed in these environments:

- **Hard soil**: usually dry and difficult to dig in; shallow soil with an underlying layer of rock
- **Rocky soil**: filled with pebbles and stones
- **Thorny soil**: filled with weeds
- **Good soil**: dark, moist soil filled with nutrients

For best results and greater involvement, have a Sunday school class take on this project. They can spend a few weeks reading this scripture passage and watching the seeds grow. You can also videotape their project and show that on a screen during the worship service.

EXTRAS:

In the children's moment, pass out seed packets for the children to take home and grow plants. Tell the parable about the seeds, and explain the plants on the altar. Thank the children for their help in providing the plants for this sermon.

ENDING:

Before the benediction, give the healthy plant in good soil to one of your parishioners, exhorting him or her to care for it with all diligence and tenderness.

WHO'S IN THE MIRROR?

2 Corinthians 3:17–18

THE MESSAGE:

1. Whom do you see when you look in the mirror? Do you see yourself, blemishes and all? Do you see something that is not yet there? Describe the television show *Extreme Makeover* and all the other makeover shows on TV. Is it any wonder that society is obsessed with the "makeover" craze? As disciples of Christ, we are called to a life of extreme makeover not to our outward bodies but to our inward souls.

2. The scripture setting (see THE BACKGROUND).

3. Describe Paul's appearance.

4. Whom do you see when you look in the mirror? Do you reflect Jesus to others and to yourself?

5. An invitation. Look at yourself in a mirror for one full minute without looking away.

6. Pray for the people while they look into the mirror. Pray for their reflection to be like Jesus.

THE BACKGROUND:

The setting for the second letter to the Corinthians was the city of Corinth, which was called "the Bridge of Greece." The city, located on Cape Malea, was known for its dangerous waters and for the Corinth Canal. Corinth became a powerful and wealthy city because this canal made it possible for commerce to travel through

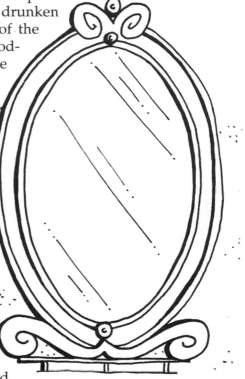

the area. Corinth also had a reputation for loose, immoral, and drunken behavior. It was the place of the temple of Aphrodite, the goddess of love. This temple employed one thousand priestesses who were temple prostitutes. It was the "Las Vegas strip" of Greece and was actually called "the Lounge of Greece."[16]

It was here that Paul started a church! And this church had been doing well at spreading light and salt in the dark and tasteless areas of the city. But in time, new leaders came forth who questioned some of the basics of Christian living. They wanted Christians to live by the rules and regulations of the Jewish law rather than in the freedom of the gospel that Paul preached. Paul countered these charges and called for Christians to reflect the glory of Christ.

In an ancient book called *The Acts of Paul and Thecla*, written about 200 CE, Paul is described as a "man of little stature, thin-haired upon the head, crooked in the legs, of good state of body, with eyebrows meeting, and with nose somewhat hooked." He was also said to be "full of grace, for sometimes he appeared like a man and sometimes he had the face of an angel."[17]

THE CREATIVE AVENUE:

Mirrors are common articles that we carry. Women often have one in their purses. At the end of the message, have everyone pull out a mirror and look into it. Have the ushers pass out small mirrors to those who do not have one. You might need a mirror for half of your congregation.

As you pray for people, ask them to keep their eyes open and to look into the mirror. Pray for Jesus to be seen in their faces as He fills their hearts and souls with joy.

EXTRAS:

For the children's moment, talk about whom we see in the mirror, using a rather large mirror for the children to look into. Let them have fun looking at the reflection of their faces. Then have a second mirror with Jesus' picture taped on it. Show them how we can reflect Jesus in the mirror.

ENDING:

During the benediction, remind people that, to the world, Jesus looks like them. Encourage them to go forth and reflect God's glory in all they say and do.

MUSTARD-SEED FAITH OR ITTY-BITTY FAITH

Matthew 17:20

THE MESSAGE:

God doesn't ask for much from us—just faith as small as a mustard seed. With that barely-able-to-be-seen faith, God can work wonders with our lives. Don't worry that you don't have enough faith. Just give God what faith you already have.

1. Describe mustard-seed qualities, focusing on how this seed turns into a plant that is often mistaken for a tree.

2. Describe small things (babies, Chihuahua dogs, petite grandmas, banana seeds, grains of sand, raindrops, and embryos).

3. Discuss faith and mountain-moving mustard seeds.

4. Tell a couple of stories about little steps of faith that produced big results.

5. Encourage people to have faith: even just a little!

THE BACKGROUND:

When I went to Israel, we stopped in the town of Bethany, and our guide pointed out a mustard seed plant, which looked like a tree! He explained that although it is one of the largest plants, it comes from one of the smallest seeds. Mustard seeds are from the cruciferous vegetable family, much like broccoli and brussels sprouts. They are mentioned in Sanskrit writings that date back five thousand years. They can be traced back to many areas including the Mediterranean regions of Jesus' life.[18]

THE CREATIVE AVENUE:

Mustard seeds are amazing things to hold in your hands. They are so tiny that if you have the slightest vision problem, it might be hard to see the individual seed! During this message, give everyone a mustard seed. You can do this in various ways, so pick the one that works best in your setting.

1. Scotch-tape a seed in the top right-hand corner of every bulletin.

2. Hand out a seed to each person who enters the sanctuary, instructing them to hold it throughout the service.

3. Have the ushers pass a bowl of seeds down the rows, and ask everyone to take one out of the bowl.

4. Wrap one seed in a square of Scotch tape and pass those out to the people. This makes it easier to hold on to the itty-bitty seeds.

EXTRAS:

Display a large potted tree in the front of the sanctuary. The mustard seed is a plant that is so large it looks like a tree. Point out the size of the potted tree as a comparison to the plant that grows from this small seed.

ENDING:

End with a song about faith.

EIGHTEEN SEEDS

THE LINEN BELT AND DIRTY LAUNDRY

Jeremiah 13:1–14

THE MESSAGE:

The theme of this message is that when we refuse to follow God, our lives become as useless as a mildewed, rotted linen belt that has been buried for a long time. Pay attention to God's ways so that you can have a life that is fully utilized for God's glory.

1. Dirty laundry. There are three kinds of laundry: regular dirty, stained laundry that needs a good soaking, and mildewed laundry that can infect the whole load/basket.

2. The scripture story: Tell the story of Jeremiah's linen belt that became mildewed and rotted.

3. A warning against the sin of pride. God was speaking to the Israelites about the infusion of pride and about following idols. He reminds them they will become like the rotted and mildewed linen belt—good for nothing!

4. Sin comes in all stages of decay. Compare sin to the laundry basket. The worst form of sin is when it affects the whole community.

5. The grace of Jesus over the infestations of mildew. While mildewed laundry usually needs to be thrown away, sometimes a good dose of bleach will do the job. Jesus died for our sins so that our lives can be restored to cleanliness and like-new freshness.

6. End with a story of redemption and restoration.

THE BACKGROUND:

Jeremiah was a prophet who spoke some harsh words to the people of Israel. He was trying to be God's voice to turn them from their sinful ways and to bring them back into a right relationship with their Creator. His words were a burden to him, and he sometimes complained to God that he had nothing but bad news for the people. But still he warned them as God asked him to, hoping they would change their ways. In this particular passage, Jeremiah is warning the people against pride. They were worshiping idols, going their own merry way without listening to God's direction for their lives.

In Psalm 51 David asks God to "create a clean heart" in him after he has committed adultery with Bathsheba. The New International Version of this psalm gives at least three terms for a person's wrongdoing: "transgression" (going against authority), "iniquity" (straying away in a perverse action), and "sin" (missing the mark, or being totally off-base as a Christian person). There are also at least three terms for removing the stain of sin: "blot out" (like using Wite-Out to erase a mistake written down in a book), "wash" (suggests that a stain is set in the fabric and needs a good scrubbing), and "cleanse" (shows a sin that has contaminated a group of people and may make one unfit for worship in the Old Testament sense).

THE CREATIVE AVENUE:

Use three laundry baskets as examples of layers of filth. Make the first basket full of crumpled, dirty clothes. For the second basket, spray brown blobs on the laundry (use old rags). For the third basket, spray the items with black, moldy-looking stains. Line the baskets in the front of the sanctuary where they are clearly visible.

This is a visual-only metaphor. You can point out the baskets as you talk about the different kinds of laundry, or you can just let people figure things out for themselves. If you have cameras and a big sanctuary, project the baskets up on the screens as you are talking about them.

EXTRAS:

Focus your songs on the topic of cleansing, being whiter than snow, redemption, and forgiveness.

ENDING:

Remind people of the sweet, fresh smell of clean laundry. Describe it in such a way that they can smell it for themselves. Perhaps remind them of hanging out laundry to dry in fresh air, or of pulling it out of the dryer. Let them breathe in the freshness of forgiveness that comes from the grace of God.

THE BREAD-MAKER GOD
Holy Communion

Luke 22:14–20

THE MESSAGE:

Holy Communion is celebrated in Christian churches all over the world, and it connects us to God and to the community of believers. This sermon will connect us to the breads of our childhood, to our histories, and to the God who shapes us into a people who are changed by His grace.

1. Invite people to receive Holy Communion as described in THE CREATIVE AVENUE.

2. Tell the story of the Lord's Supper.

3. Tell why you chose a particular bread. For example, if you picked tortillas, talk about your connection to the Hispanic culture, including a story that comes out of that culture.

4. Remembering. Jesus gave us this ritual so that we could remember Him. Memory makes real what we cannot see. Memory involves all of our senses. Memory shapes and forms us for the present and for our future. Tell a story of how you remember someone who meant a lot to you, and how that memory of the loved one shaped you.

5. Connection during World Communion Sunday: Christians all over the world are celebrating Communion together. Communion connects us.

6. Covenant: Holy Communion as a covenant, or agreement, between our Savior and us.

7. End with a story of God's self-giving that changes your life.

THE BACKGROUND:

Communion is one of our most sacred acts as communities of Christ. It is how we gather to remember and receive in the present what Christ did for us in the past. Communion connects us to one another and to Jesus Christ. It is the means of grace that mysteriously brings us forgiveness, healing, restoration, and vitalization.

Communion reminds us of the way that God has fed us and provided for us over the course of time. When God provided manna, the "what is it?" of the desert, the people ate and had enough. And now, Jesus provides the sustenance of His own body, which is enough for our daily nurture. It is the soul food, the cultural-connect to the Savior, and the nourishment for Christian living.

As a people who receive Holy Sustenance together, we remember to set aside our differences and to love one another as Christ loved us when He laid down His life for ours. There is no greater love, and we too can walk in that love with the ordinary folks who walk beside us.

THE CREATIVE AVENUE:

This message is a good one for World Communion Sunday or a special Holy Communion service. I first saw this done at a chapel service at Claremont School of Theology. Ask one of the laypersons to make bread for the Communion table. Instruct her or him to make it multicolored. This can be done by splitting the dough into four balls and adding food coloring to each one. Then roll out each ball into a long, snakelike tube and twist the tubes together. Once baked, this colorful bread represents all the people of the world. Use this bread as the bread you break from when you say the Words of Institution. The people will be surprised by the colors that show when you hold up the broken loaf.

Next, set the Communion table with breads from many different cultures and places in life. For example, have a plate of tortillas to represent the Hispanic population, rice cakes to represent Asians, cookies to represent children, rye bread to represent Germanic folk, and corn bread to represent people who work the fields of the earth. Be as creative as possible, choosing breads that represent your community and the ancestors of your community.

Begin your service with Holy Communion (putting it up front draws attention to this special moment). When you break the colorful main loaf of bread, also stop and break the other kinds of bread, mentioning the people groups they represent. Invite people to come to the altar table, pick the bread of their choice, and dip it in the grape juice (have several cups of juice on the table).

Someone in your congregation will be honored to set this special table and will do so with great artistic flair. When I did this one, I moved the altar table down into the center of the congregation. You could also put it somewhere close to the place where people enter the sanctuary. When you speak the Words of Institution, move down to the Communion table.

EXTRAS:

Explain why the bread represents the body and the juice represents the blood of Jesus to your children during a children's moment. Children understand how Communion helps us remember what Jesus did for us. Take a moment to explain one more aspect of this ritual to them. Each time you stop to teach children about Communion, they will experience it in a deeper way.

ENDING:

During the benediction, invite people to hold hands as a reminder that they are a community of Christ-followers as you lead them in a closing prayer.

TWENTY SEEDS

THE SECRET CHORD

Judges 13–16; 2 Samuel 11–12; Psalm 51:15

Unseal my lips, O Lord, that I may praise you.
(Ps. 51:15)

THE MESSAGE:

This is a message that is an intersection of two stories. Both stories are raw with real life, real sin, and real redemption. The song entitled "Hallelujah," by Rufus Wainwright, is the connector for this message. You can find the song on the *Shrek* sound track (Dreamworks, 2001) and also on the *Lifted Songs of the Spirit* album distributed through Starbucks (Sony/Hear Music, 2002). Listen to the song as you prepare for this message.

1. Explain the Philistines (Samson and Delilah story setup)

2. Explain "Nazirites."

3. Tell the story of Delilah and Samson.

4. Tell the story of David and Bathsheba. In Psalm 51, David repents and prays:

> *Create in me a clean heart…*
> *Make me willing to obey you…*
> *Unseal my lips, O Lord,*
> *that I may praise you.*

David is saying, "I can't even go to worship and offer sacrifices (because of my sin). And the sacrifice You want is a broken and repentant heart. That is my sacrifice to You, Lord, that I can praise You."

5. Things that keep you from praising God. Name things that separate us from God in such a way that we cannot worship and praise.

6. "Hallelujah" (see THE CREATIVE AVENUE).

7. Concluding connecting story of praising God through the hard times.

THE BACKGROUND:

If you look through a basic Bible dictionary, you will find these (and other) interesting bits of information and history that may add to your storytelling:

1. The Philistines. These were a people who lived in the southwest part of Palestine and were known as the "Sea Peoples." They invaded Egypt around 1188 BCE by land and sea, fighting against the famous Ramses III. They traveled in ships that had a curved keel with a bird head at the bow (you've probably seen pictures of these). The warriors wore feathered headdresses, which increased their stature and their intimidation factor. They were also experts at metal processing, making coats of armor, helmets, leg protectors, spears, and shields. They were the main enemy and threat to Israel during the time of the judges and during Samson's day.

2. The Nazirites. These were people who were dedicated to God. The term denotes consecration, devotion, and separation. People became Nazirites by taking a vow for a limited period of time or by being placed under a lifetime vow by their parents. Nazirites had to refrain from all alcohol, from contact with the dead, and from cutting their hair. These were outward signs of inward dedication to God. In the Bible, some Nazirites include Samson, John the Baptist, and Paul.

3. Delilah. She was probably a Philistine. Her name means "with long hair hanging down." We know she enticed Samson to tell the secret of his strength, and she betrayed him to the Philistines by cutting his hair and turning him over to them while he slept.

4. Samson. His name means "of the sun." He was the last of the major judges over Israel and lived around 1100 BCE. Samson was from the tribe of Dan and was a lifelong Nazirite. He was a young man who was headstrong and seemed to have little self-control. His major life crises were always because of Philistine women. He did not ever free his people from the Philistines, but he caused the Philistines a major setback when he died and destroyed their temple along with crowds of people. His death was a last act of sacrifice to God.

5. David and Bathsheba. The Bible is great about handling the real difficulties of life straight on, especially when looking at our heroes. The reason the Bible can be so forthright and not hide the mistakes of our heroes is that the Bible is not about people as much as it is about God. No matter how great we are, or what titles we hold, or what our income status is, the Bible looks directly at our woes and then honors God's grace to forgive and rebuild.

   David, the king-hero, made a real mess out of his life. He had an affair with Bathsheba, getting her pregnant. Then he tried to cover up his mistake by enticing Bathsheba's husband, Uriah the Hittite, to sleep with her during battle time (which was against the code of soldiers in battle). Finally he resorted to having Uriah sent to the front lines of battle so that he would be killed. After all this, he took Bathsheba to be his wife. Nathan the prophet confronted him with his sin, and David saw the error of his heart and actions, crying out to God to make him clean so that he could worship and praise God again.

THE CREATIVE AVENUE:

This musical sermon incorporates the song "Hallelujah," which is weaved in and out of the message. You can do this in any way that seems to make sense to you in your formation of the sermon. What I did was have the band sing "Hallelujah" as a setup to the sermon and then come back and play the song again at the end of the message. It is a haunting number that is easy to listen to more than once. You can also have the musicians play pieces of the song as you see fit.

ENDING:

David heard a secret chord. It was the chord of grace and for-giveness—a fresh start. David, in his sin, missed being close to God so that he could worship Him. He missed the presence of the Holy One in his unclean and unholy state. May your heart be clean and your lips be free to praise Him!

TWENTY-ONE SEEDS

A CHILD'S POINT OF VIEW

Mark 10:13–16

THE MESSAGE:

This sermon is an interview with children (third through sixth grades) in an attempt to see the future of the church through their eyes. You will tell stories to and hear stories from the children.

1. A little girl saves her brother. I saw a story on TV in which a little girl was given an award for saving her younger brother. There was a fire in her home, and she got herself out and then went back in to get her little brother out of the fire. She suffered burns on her hands, but she pushed on and saved her brother. They gave her the first award given to a civilian for such bravery. Her comment was, "I was brave, and I just wanted to get my brother out."

   I sometimes look at the state of the church today and in dismay wonder how we will fare in the future. Will the children of our world come to know the Lord, or will there be a generation lost to the saving grace of Jesus Christ?

   When I think about it, I sometimes think that, like that little girl, the children will be the ones who save us as a church.

2. Introduce the children you will be interviewing. Ask them some warm-up questions. These questions might be:
   a. How old are you?
   b. What school do you go to?
   c. What is your favorite color?
   d. What animal name begins with the first letter of your name?

e. What is your favorite cartoon/TV show?

   f. Favorite teacher? Favorite pastor (ha!)?

   g. Favorite fruit?

   h. Least favorite vegetable?

   i. What sport do you play?

   j. Best brand of sneakers?

   k. Tell us about your pet.

3. Describe the children of today, sometimes called "Mosaics" or "Millennials" (see THE BACKGROUND).

4. Now interview children again with these questions:
   a. What would make the world a better place?

   b. How can we be better people?

   c. What color is love?

   d. Who is your hero?

   e. How did you learn about Jesus?

   f. What is the worst thing in the world? Why?

   g. What should we do to make the world a better place? (Asking this more than once gives a second go at an important issue.)

h. How has Jesus helped you?

i. What can we do better at church?

5. Scripture. Talk about the faith of children. Talk about Jesus' call for all people to have a child's kind of faith. Wonder why we must have faith like children in order to enter the kingdom of God.

6. Interview children again with these questions:
   a. Who is Jesus?
   b. Tell me your favorite Bible story.
   c. How did God make you?
   d. What are you really good at?
   e. Tell me about heaven.
   f. What is hell?
   g. Where does Jesus live?
   h. How can adults make things better?
   i. If Jesus were standing right here today, what do you think He would say to us?
   j. If Jesus were here today, what kinds of people would He be concerned about?

7. Tell the story of Samuel, the little boy who heard God calling in the night (see 1 Sam. 3).

8. Ask the children one more question: What would you say to me, your pastor, about God?

THE BACKGROUND:

My friend Jon Burgess sent me a wonderful interview from *60 Minutes* that describes those who are called Millennials.[19] Some interesting characteristics include:

   a. Born between 1984 and 2002
   b. The most numerous generation in American history, exceeding the Boomers by several million
   c. Eclectic lifestyles ranging from traditional to alternative
   d. Nonlinear thinkers
   e. Relationships are racially integrated

f. Internet is primary information source

g. Tend to customize and blend their faith and religious views

h. Positive self-worth

i. Want a meaningful career

j. Value education

k. Relationally driven

l. Mass media central to their experience

THE CREATIVE AVENUE:

This is a message from you AND from the children. Use interview-style conversations with them. Pick three or four very verbal children and one or two quieter ones. You will be amazed at the depth that can come from these introverted children when you invite them to talk. The children I chose were in grade school, mostly from the upper grades (third through sixth grades).

Practice this sermon the night before with the children, complete with microphones. The children need to get used to hearing their voices projected over the sound system.

For some of the deeper questions, or the question about their favorite Bible story, you can practice these beforehand. This gives you a feel of what's coming and helps you to ask the question in a way that encourages the children to talk.

Be a good listener. Be attentive to the speakers. Smile and make them feel comfortable.

EXTRAS:

If you have a vision for children's ministry in your church, this would be a great time to remind people of that call and to pass out the vision in writing (perhaps on a refrigerator magnet or on a bookmark) for them to place in a prominent place.

ENDING:

During the benediction, have the children stand up with you and give the blessing with you, along with the sign of the cross given in unison. (Practice this with them beforehand!)

I CAN ONLY IMAGINE

Luke 4:14–30

THE MESSAGE:

Theme: Jesus proclaimed that He was the very presence of God standing before the people in His hometown of Nazareth. Many didn't believe Him and tried to kill Him. How often do we fail to see God among us or to live heaven on earth?

1. Introduction: I was sitting in my Arizona room, reading the Bible and preparing for this sermon. As I sat there with my Bible on my lap, my daughter Natalie was in the office nearby, IMing her friends and singing along to music. The words of the song she was singing began to float into my brain, and then into my soul…

2. Have someone sing the first part of "I Can Only Imagine," by Bart Millard, found on Mercy Me's *Almost There* album (Word/Curb Records, 2002).

3. Heaven. This song is about heaven, imagining what it is like to be in the presence of God for the first time. This is what heaven is: being fully in the presence of God—face-to-face—in all the glory and awesomeness, in all the love and wonder, in all the beauty. Heaven is standing before God with no barriers.

   Describe flying in the clouds on an airplane, and then describe your view of heaven. What will you do? Will you fall before Jesus? Will you dance? Will you shout for joy, or do cartwheels? How will you respond?

4. Tell the scripture story.

5. Describe a daily situation in which what you hoped would be "heavenly" actually turned out to be far from the ideal of heaven on earth. I described how we always hope for a "perfect" family in a perfect town in perfect slow time on a perfect Christmas Day. This ideal rarely comes true.

6. Heaven on earth. Describe the scripture passage when Jesus goes to His hometown, but the people do not recognize Him for who He is. How many of us also meet Jesus every day— meet heaven on earth—but do not see Him for who He is?

7. Describe worship as a moment of heaven touching earth. When we worship God, we give Him our praise, our sacrifice, our words, and our deeds. God promises to meet us in this moment and because of this connection, it is like a moment of heaven and earth becoming one.

8. Tell of a moment when you experienced heaven on earth.

9. "I Can Only Imagine." The vocalist sings the ending of this song. You can have other singers join in one line at a time (layering effect), and then invite the congregation to sing along.

THE BACKGROUND:

Jesus had just returned from forty days of temptation. He experienced forty days of hunger, thirst, and being tempted by the devil. And after surviving that episode, Jesus went down to His hometown area and began preaching to people along the way. People were amazed, and rumors spread quickly. "You gotta hear this guy!" People praised Him everywhere He went. So He went to His hometown of Nazareth. On the Sabbath, He was invited to read the Scripture. He stood and asked for the Isaiah scroll and read the passage:

> *The Spirit of the Lord is upon me,*
> *for he has appointed me to preach Good News to the poor.*
> *He has sent me to proclaim*
> *that captives will be released,*
> *that the blind will see,*
> *that the downtrodden will be freed from their oppressors,*
> *and that the time of the Lord's favor has come.*
> *(Luke 4:18–19)*

Then He rolled up the scroll and sat down to preach. And with everyone looking at Him, He said,

> *This Scripture has come true today before your very eyes!*
> *(Luke 4:21)*

Jesus was telling them something very important. He was saying that the time of the Messiah—the awaited Savior—was now. He was telling them that He was the One, that He was God, that they were standing in the presence of God, and that before their eyes was heaven on earth! The kingdom of God was now!

The reaction of the crowd was varied. Some were amazed by the words of grace that came out of His mouth. Others were just spittin' mad! "Who does this guy think he is? Isn't that Joseph's boy? Doesn't his sister still live among us—the one on Main and Ninth Street? Who does he think he is, saying he's the One?"

And so they chased Him to the cliff at the edge of town, intending to push Him over the edge and kill Him, but Jesus snuck out between the crowds and left His hometown behind.

You see, they didn't recognize Jesus in His hometown, and I wonder sometimes if we do any better today. Think about it. If the man sitting next to you got up and read today's passage and then said to you, "That's me! I'm the one! I'm God sitting next to you!" what would you say? Would you believe him, or would you move over one seat? Jesus was trying to tell the people that heaven is now. It is not some distant, faraway place, but it is also now. Heaven exists in the middle of your trials, your troubles, and your struggles. Jesus, the very Son of God, is right before you and can make a difference in your life if you will only recognize Him!

How many of us go throughout our lives without Jesus? How many of us know that He's out there somewhere, but we never fall down in His presence to worship the One who loves us and forgives us? How many of us never call on Him in times of distress? How often do we come to church out of habit, never connecting with the One who quietly waits to hear His name spoken on our lips and in our hearts? Who among us would be in favor of driving Him off the bridge interchange of Loop 101 because we don't get what He is saying? Heaven on earth: A preposterous idea? Or a breath of fresh air in a sin-sick world?

THE CREATIVE AVENUE:

This is another musical sermon. Music connected with Scripture is more powerful than we can ever begin to understand. It takes what you are trying to say and moves people to a much deeper level of understanding and connection. This particular musical sermon is a weave, utilizing music in the beginning and the end of the message.

Find a great singer for this one, and let your instrumentalists back up the singer.

EXTRAS:

In the last singing of the song toward the end of the sermon, you can have a group of singers step onto stage one by one (adding a singer with each line) to create depth and variety. This also helps the congregation to join in freely and to sing along with this popular tune.

ENDING:

I would invite the people to stand and sing along with the end of this song as a prayer. Then go right into a prayer, calling on God to help us recognize heaven on earth.

TEARS IN A BOTTLE

Psalm 56:8–13

THE MESSAGE:

This message will help us to see tears as God sees them: as treasures worth keeping in bottles. Every tear is a drop of love expressed outwardly. Tears of joy and tears of pain all come from the source of love.

1. Describe a time when you cried.

2. Collections. Describe things we collect (china, shoes, ceramic teapots, angels, tools, books, etc.). We like to collect things we love. God collects tears.

3. Tears are outward symbols of inward grief. Grief happens because of a loss of love. If we did not love, we would not cry for what was lost. So, tears are really signs of our love. When someone is grieving, it is a sign that love existed. Often people are ashamed of their tears, but I like to remind people that those very tears are signs of deep love, which is nothing to be ashamed about!

4. Grieving process. Explain the grieving process and the part that tears play in the healing from grief.

5. Tears. Explain the biological function of tears (see THE BACKGROUND).

6. Biblical explanation of "tears in your bottle."

7. Scripture. Expound on David's expression of grief and his hope to be rescued and to be able to walk in the life-giving light of God's presence.

8. Describe our "Bank of Tears." It's not that we plan to cry, or even that we want to! But if God holds our tears in a bottle—as in a Heavenly Tear Bank—how precious they must be to God! What does your "Tear Bank" look like? Tears, like love, are never wasted. Count your treasure in heaven just as God does.

THE BACKGROUND:

Tears are made from proteins, enzymes, lipids, metabolites, and electrolytes. The amount of proteins present in tears when one cries because of an irritant in the eye is different from the amount present when one cries for emotional reasons.[20] Tears are 98 percent water. They have three functions: (1) Basic or basal tears provide needed lubrication for the eyes, (2) reflex tears come when an irritant is present or at a time of trauma to the eye and have the protective role, and (3) emotional tears are outward expressions of a variety of feelings.[21]

Tear bottles were found in Egypt and Middle-Eastern societies and were quite common in the ancient Roman period.[22] Mourners would use small glass bottles to collect tears in and then place these bottles in the tomb with the deceased. Sometimes mourners were even paid to be professional grievers, and those who cried the loudest and collected the most tears were highly respected. According to the legend, the more tears, the higher the value of the lost loved one.

This tradition reappeared during Victorian times. They added a new component by leaving the stopper off the bottle. When the evaporation process had dried up all the tears, the mourning period was over.

Some American Civil War stories include tear bottles, which women kept until their husbands returned from war and then proudly showed them to the men as symbols of great love.[23]

THE CREATIVE AVENUE:

This is a "show-and-tell" sermon. The idea is to create "tears in a bottle" in little containers to count how many tears fill up a small vial or small bottle. You can pass that bottle around for each person to see, perhaps with the number of tears you counted written in bold black on the outside of the bottle.

First find a small vial. Then drop water into the bottle with an eyedropper. This allows you to count the "tears" as you fill it up.

EXTRAS:

You could also bring in your favorite collection to show. For example, if you collect teapots, place several of them in a prominent and visible position. Tell people a little about how you started your collection, where your pieces come from, and something of their emotional or financial value.

ENDING:

Blessing of tears. Pray a blessing on the tears that have been shed, the tears that are washing away the pain, and the tears that will bring healing in the future.

ALTARS

Joshua 3–4; Exodus 20:24b

THE MESSAGE:

Altars are places where we remember a special move of God in our lives. We still need to create these spaces of memory—places where we can tell our children and our grandchildren what God has done for us.

1. I have a collection of rocks. They are just plain pebbles that I have picked up in various places when I wanted to remember something. For example, I have a rock from a great vacation spot on the ocean, I have a rock from the grounds of my college, and I have a rock from a retreat place where God moved my soul. I keep these rocks in my office to remind me of what God has done in my life.

2. Describe the purpose of altars in the Bible: to be places of memory for what God has done.

3. Tell the story of Moses building an altar after receiving the Ten Commandments (or pick some other story in the Bible about building an altar as a remembrance of God).

4. Tell the story of Joshua and the parting of the Jordan River. Explain the memorial that was built so that the next generations could hear how God worked in their midst.

5. Remind people of the things God has done in their lives. Start by telling something that God has done for you that has changed your life.

6. Invite people to pick up the rocks under their seats and to take a moment to remember one great thing God has done for them. Have them write on the stones a word or two that bring back that memory, and then add their names if they wish. Ask them to bring the rocks to the altar when they are finished, stopping for a moment to kneel and pray a prayer of gratitude.

7. Encourage people to tell the stories of how God has worked in their lives to their children, coworkers, friends, and family. Remind them to be witnesses and memorials—living altars of remembrance.

THE BACKGROUND:

Altars were built as places of sacrifice and as places to remember a theophany, a place where God had appeared. Altars were built with stones in their raw form until Solomon's Temple changed the setting. The altar that Joshua built after crossing the Jordan River was a reminder that God broke through in their history to provide a way.[24]

When Joshua and the people built the memorial, they intended it to serve as a place for conversations about how this amazing event occurred. In essence, the stones were meant to peak the curiosity of the next generation and to prompt those who had been present to tell the story.

THE CREATIVE AVENUE:

The idea for this message is for your congregation to build an altar of remembrance together. I started out by inviting the Confirmation Class to go out on our church property and find a rock. Some of them brought large boulders, and some brought little pebbles. Then I led a study inviting them to remember what God has done in their lives. I asked them to take a permanent marker and write on the rocks the one word they wanted to remember from that experience. I also asked them to write their first names on the rocks. Then we took the rocks into the sanctuary and built an altar, a pile of stones.

If you choose to start with an existing altar, begin the sermon by explaining the pile of rocks. During the message there will be a time when each of the people will be invited to write on a rock a memory, along with their name, and to carry that rock to the front of the church and add it to the pile. When this is happening, ask some musicians to provide some background music. Encourage people to stop for a moment to pray as they add their rocks to the pile.

I live in Arizona, and we have an abundance of rocks. You might have to go somewhere to get rocks—a riverbed, a forest, a lakeshore, etc. Whatever the case may be, have someone gather rocks and place one rock under each seat prior to the start of the service. Then pass out permanent markers, asking the people to share them.

EXTRAS:

It would be great to find a way to highlight your church altar this week. Center it in a more visible place, perhaps closer to the people. If possible, move the seats around and put the altar in the center of the space instead of at the front. Have someone with artistic talent decorate the altar with simple and earthen décor, using only raw materials and natural forms. You could also preach from the center of the church, near the altar, to highlight this sacred memorial tool.

ENDING:

During the benediction, bless the stories and the storytellers, the memories and the memory-makers.

MASTERPIECE

Ephesians 2:10

THE MESSAGE:

1. Masterpiece. Tell of a masterpiece (famous painting) that you have seen and how you felt when you saw it.

2. Show three or four masterpieces on a screen, and tell their stories and the history behind them.

3. We are God's masterpieces! Comment on the scripture passage where Paul states that we also are masterpieces.

4. Challenge the people to see themselves and their lives as God's masterpieces. How does that change them? What do they look like? What is their purpose?

THE BACKGROUND:

Some paintings to consider:

- Vincent van Gogh, *The Sunflowers*
- Vincent van Gogh, *Church at Auvers*
- Vincent van Gogh, *Starry Night*[25]
- Pierre-Auguste Renoir, *The Great Boulevards*
- Paul Cézanne, *Chestnut Trees at the Jas de Bouffan in Winter*
- Claude Monet, *The Japanese Bridge*[26]
- Leonardo da Vinci, *Mona Lisa*
- Michelangelo Buonarroti, Sistine Chapel frescoes
- Paul Gauguin, *Woman with a Flower*[27]

THE CREATIVE AVENUE:

One of the few video presentations in this book, this message focuses on well-known paintings and gives some commentary on three or four of them in order to bring understanding to the words:

For we are God's masterpiece. (Eph. 2:10)

So, you will need to prepare a video or slide show of famous paintings and show them on a screen. You could show them at the beginning of the message or spread them throughout the sermon. As you show each masterpiece, I would recommend that you tell some of the stories behind the works of art. For example, how long did it take the artist to create the painting? Tell some of the life story of the artist. What did the work of art mean to the artist? What is its financial value? Where is it today?

EXTRAS:

Invite the artists in your congregation and community to display their works of art in your lobby for this service.

ENDING:

God created beauty and art. You are God's pride and joy. You are God's masterpiece!

DON'T LOOK BACK!

Genesis 19:26

THE MESSAGE:

1. Tell of a time when you struggled with going forward, pining for what you left behind.

2. Tell the story of Lot and Lot's wife. This is a long and delicate story. The story is worth telling, but be careful for the children in your church. Encourage the adults to go home and read the rest! But do tell as much as possible because the story of seeking to follow God in the midst of evil is relevant even today!

3. Discuss the reason our eyes are in the front of our heads, our ears face forward, and our rear ends are behind us.

4. Remind folks how hard it is to walk forward while looking backward. We have a tendency to trip, stumble, bump into things, and fall flat on our faces.

5. Moving forward. Discuss the possibilities in life as we move forward. Remind people that God is always at work redeeming our lives and creating a new thing.

THE BACKGROUND:

The story is set in the city of Sodom, and God sent Lot and his wife and family out of the city, away from the path of evil. Lot had been raised by his uncle Abraham after his father's death, and they separated ways so that the employees would quit bickering. Lot got to choose the way to go, and he chose the fertile Jordan Valley.

But appearances can be deceiving, for the history of this area was sordid. This is the place where the people tried to reach God by their works when they built the tower of Babel. This is the place where Abraham's father, Terah, gave up on his dream and settled. And we all know this is the place where the infamous city of Sodom became known as a wicked place. Yet Lot chose to live here, in the green valley.

Things were not as good as they seemed in the Jordan Valley. The neighbors weren't neighborly, the friends weren't friendly, and the life was a little bit too lively. So when wickedness abounded, God sent Lot and his family away to safety. But Lot's wife couldn't run forward without looking backward. And so she turned into a pillar of salt, frozen in time in the looking-back position of life. Not a way to live, by the way.

THE CREATIVE AVENUE:

Sometimes a small action is enough to create impact and emphasis. That is what will happen with this sermon. The idea is for you to literally *look back* several times during the sermon. At first, people will not notice anything, but after a few times, they will get it. You can look back in the following ways:

1. Glance over your shoulder.
2. Turn around and stare for a good length of time behind you.
3. Look down to the ground, slightly behind you.
4. Look up and over your shoulder toward the ceiling.
5. If you are adventuresome, lean over and look through your legs.

Start out with the smaller gestures of looking back, and then use the more dramatic ones toward the end of your message.

Don't verbally acknowledge your behaviors. Let your body speak this point.

EXTRAS:

For the children's moment, have a child walk forward while looking backward. Walk with her or him to provide safety.

ENDING:

There are many times in life that we have a choice. We can either go forward with faith or look back with longing. My advice to you is, "Don't look back!"

TWENTY-SEVEN SEEDS

ENOUGH! (ON PUTRID MANNA)

Exodus 16; Luke 12:22–31

THE MESSAGE:

Begin the sermon with one of your congregation's musicians singing the song "Enough," by Greg Ferguson (found on the *Enough* album, by Willow Creek Community Church; see www.willowcreek.com/resources).

1. Have you ever been stuffed? Full to the brim? No more room for even a bite of dessert? Describe this feeling with your own story.

2. The promise of enough is throughout the Bible. Talk about the fear we have of "not enough" and about Jesus' words in Luke 12:22–31.

3. Tell the scripture story of manna, focusing on how the Israelites were given enough but not more than was needed. Tell what happened when they gathered more manna than they needed.

4. Address the moral issue of poverty in the face of overabundance. Perhaps tell a story of someone who is addressing this issue in a positive way (e.g., feeding the homeless).

5. Address the ways we want "more than enough" in terms of success, power, recognition, etc.

6. Invite the people to close their eyes and hear the song "Enough" one more time, using it as a prayer to God.

7. Pray.

THE BACKGROUND:

Manna, often called "food from heaven," was what God gave to the Israelites during their years in the desert. The term "manna" probably comes from the question the people had when they saw it: "What is it?" Manna foreshadows Christ as the Bread of Life.[28]

Each person was told to pick up one omer of manna per day. An omer is 2.08 quarts.[29]

THE CREATIVE AVENUE:

The song "Enough" will be the central focus of this message. Have someone sing this song before the message, and then have it sung again toward the end of your sermon. During the second singing of the song, ask people to close their eyes and listen to the song as a prayer. After the song ends, lead the congregation in a prayer.

EXTRAS:

Have a two-quart pitcher (a half gallon) of powdered milk or baby cereal to show the people how much manna they were allowed per day. This will add visual impact. Most of us eat more than that in one day . . . oops!

ENDING:

End this service by praying for the people to know that God is enough.

TWENTY-EIGHT SEEDS

SHUFFLE

The Gospels—Life of Jesus

THE MESSAGE:

Tell the story of Jesus's life, death, and resurrection. Pick several highlights of His life, and tell about them. You might include the following events:

1. Jesus'd mom and dad meet and become engaged. Mary is pregnant and goes to visit her aunt Elizabeth.

2. Jesus is born in all glory.

3. Jesus is tempted and spends forty days in a struggle with the devil.

4. Jesus calls the disciples.

5. Jesus turns water into wine at Cana.

6. Jesus heals a blind man.

7. Jesus feeds the five thousand.

8. Jesus walks on water.

9. Jesus speaks out against the religious authorities.

10. Jesus raises Lazarus from the dead.

11. Jesus is betrayed, arrested, and crucified.

12. Jesus rises from the dead.

13. Jesus speaks to followers and tells them to "go and make disciples."

THE BACKGROUND:

You know these stories, and your resource is the Gospels. Pick one Gospel, and tell Jesus' life story as seen through the eyes of that writer.

THE CREATIVE AVENUE:

I got this idea while walking and listening to my iPod. I had it on "shuffle song" mode, which picks songs out of my list and plays them in a random order. The disorderly mix seemed to speak to me in a different way, and so I thought about telling a very familiar story out of order. When we do this, we will hear things differently than we do when we hear the familiar linear approach.

I encourage you to pick six or seven events of Jesus' life to highlight who He is. Then tell those events out of order. For example, put the Resurrection event in the middle of the message and the birth event right after the Resurrection. You get the point. This feels a little uncomfortable, but go with it and see how the people respond.

You may want to tell people that you will be preaching about the life of Jesus and that the events of the story will be out of order. If you want, you could have the events written on paper and have people guess the proper order. Then at the end give them the correct linear sequence. Doing this could be fun, or it could distract them from listening. You decide which is best for your setting.

EXTRAS:

During the children's moment, show children the "shuffle songs" tool on an iPod. Explain what it does, and tell them the sermon will be like a "shuffle sermon." Have them guess how things really happened in Jesus' life.

ENDING:

Sometimes we have to mix things up because it gives us a new perspective. I hope you had a new insight into the life of your Savior today. Remember, the most important message of His life is that He loved you so much that He chose to be in relationship with you, forgive you, and conquer death for you. Go and love likewise!

STILL

1 Kings 19:9–13a

THE MESSAGE:

1. Discuss the evolution of noise in our society. We are inundated with sound from early morning to late evening. We have the TV, the radio, traffic—all sounds of life that seem to fill our ears every moment of every day. Perhaps what we need to better hear God are periods of silence.

2. State the problem: we often need to hear God's voice of direction in our lives, but we don't have enough still moments to be able to listen. We are distracted from hearing God by the activities and noises of our daily lives.

3. Tell a personal story of experiencing silence and a connection to God. I told a story about being on a boat at night when we turned off the motor, lay back on the seats to see the stars, and felt an amazing connection with the God of the universe who cares for us!

4. Tell the story of Elijah when he hears God in the still, small voice.

5. Invite the congregation to listen to the sound of silence as they pray.

THE BACKGROUND:

Elijah was a ninth-century BCE prophet to the northern reign of Israel. We know that he dressed strangely, jogged fast, hung out in caves, and probably enjoyed the outdoors. He spoke for the One

God, versus the many gods of the day. He spoke out even when it meant that he disagreed with the rulers, kings, and advisers. After Elijah heard God in the still, small voice, he spoke the downfall of the current king and called for reform in his beloved Israel.[30]

THE CREATIVE AVENUE:

This message will be sprinkled with periods of stillness, silence, or soft music. To see how God spoke to Elijah in the still voice or the soft whisper, we too can experience a quiet spot for listening to God.

As you formulate your words, also form periods of stillness. Create three, maybe four such periods. The first quiet moment is accompanied by the soft sound of music. Choose this music well, specifically finding a piece that brings a sense of tranquility. The next period of quiet can be accompanied by sight but not sound. For example, create a video of peaceful settings. If you do not have the ability to utilize video projection, substitute another quiet sound, like a single voice humming "Amazing Grace." The third period of stillness is absolute silence. Give people time to pray and listen to God, seeking the still, small voice that can speak to their lives.

If you have the capability to do a video project, this could be a good sermon for de-layering. Layering is adding on forms to create surprise and depth. But in this instance you can de-layer, or deconstruct. Start with an amazing video of peaceful scenes layered with music that moves the heart and soul. Then show only the video. Then play the same music without visuals. Finally, provide a moment of complete silence without audio or visual aids.

EXTRAS:

For the children's moment, try talking in a loud voice, in a regular voice, and in a whisper. See which "voice" the children remember the most, and then explain how God got Elijah's attention through a whisper.

ENDING:

End this message with a great pause. Just stop talking for a moment, but keep looking at the people and engaging them with your eyes and body language. Then when they start to look a little uncomfortable, whisper, "Amen!"

PASSING THE MANTLE

2 Kings 2:1–18

THE MESSAGE:

1. Talk about a person who has mentored you, and describe how you are covered by his or her legacy.

2. Describe "mantles" in the Old Testament.

3. Tell the story of Elijah passing the mantle to Elisha.

4. Discuss the value of learning from the experiences of others and receiving wisdom not earned.

5. Talk about the time you were ordained and specifically about the laying on of hands in blessing and the putting on of stoles (or another object, if this is not your tradition).

6. Talk about the priesthood of all believers, and remind the people that they carry the mantle of this church to pass on the gospel to their communities.

7. Walk out as you are closing with #6, and place your stole over someone's shoulders, inviting the rest of the congregation to put the ribbons in their bulletins over their shoulders. Then encourage them to hang the ribbons as a reminder in a prominent place during this week.

THE BACKGROUND:

A mantle was an outer covering like a coat or a robe. It was made of thick wool and had two slits for arms. When I think of a mantle,

I think of the Mexican serape—a colorful outerwear that is used for warmth and protection from the weather. A mantle was usually colorful and could be what we know as Joseph's "coat of many colors." Sometimes a mantle was used to keep warm at night, and sometimes it was torn as a show of grief. It was a common article of clothing, well-known to the people of Elijah's day.[31]

THE CREATIVE AVENUE:

Many pastors wear robes with stoles. Have a special stole made for this event—one that you will pass on to a layperson in your church. You can have a special insignia (perhaps a symbol that represents your church) sewn onto a plain stole.

At the end of your message, walk down into the congregation, remove your stole, and place it on the shoulders of a layperson as a visible sign that the mantle of the priesthood is for all persons ("the priesthood of all believers").

Also, cut foot-long ribbons and place one inside each bulletin. This will represent a mantle and will be a reminder that each person has an important role to play in God's kingdom. Encourage people to place their ribbons in a prominent place (like hanging from the rearview mirror or on the refrigerator, etc.) as an ongoing reminder.

EXTRAS:

This is a great time to include a children's sermon about learning from parents and about receiving the legacy they pass down. Have special "family" stoles made to give to each child. They can simply be cut pieces of felt with a symbol pasted on. Ask a Sunday school class or some of your crafty folks to make these for you.

ENDING:

Have everyone stand up and place a hand of blessing on the shoulder of the person in the pew next to them. Then lead them in a "repeat-after-me" prayer that is a call to pass on the faith.

APPLES

Genesis 1–3

THE MESSAGE:

This message is about the times in our lives when we disobey God. It is a gentle reminder that we all sin and need to seek God's forgiveness.

1. I once climbed up into an apple tree and ate a mess of apples in one sitting, only to end up with a terrible stomachache. I crawled down from the tree and moaned and groaned in my bed, thinking I'd never eat another apple again. Maybe your parents told you not to eat too many green apples! I had ignored my mom's advice, but after that particular incident, I remembered her words more vividly! (Use this story or one from your own history.)

2. Tell about a time when you distinctly disobeyed God. Or, if you can't be that bold, tell about a time when someone else did.

3. Explain that parents give children rules to protect them from harm (not because they want to see them suffer) and that God gives us boundaries for the same reasons. Be sure to include that God's grace will catch us when we overstep the boundaries.

4. Tell the story of Adam and Eve.

5. Tell another biblical example of someone who disobeyed God—perhaps the story of Jonah.

126

6. Remind the people that God's grace is always present to restore our relationships with God and with others and that we are given second and third (etc.) chances to be obedient followers of Christ.

THE BACKGROUND:

Eve, the first woman, has a name that means "life." Adam, the first man, carries a name that means "man."[32] Adam and Eve had the privilege of walking with God in the Garden of Eden. Yet they chose to go out of the way to disobey God. As a result of their disobedience, they were removed from the garden. Adam's consequence was never-ending yard work, and Eve's was incredible pain during childbirth. Adam and Eve had to learn things the hard way because they had no one to come before them and say, "This is the way." Well, God did, but they chose not to follow God's

advice. So they experienced a son who murdered their other son. They experienced moving to a new land where they tried their best to create a society of justice, mercy, and peace, failing miserably along the way. But they were also the first to experience God's grace, forgiveness, and protection.

THE CREATIVE AVENUE:

Rev. Mary Bullis thought up this wonderful and simple way to bring the story of Adam and Eve to life. When she told me about it, the image was so vivid that I remembered it years later. I hope that this will happen for you and your congregation.

Basically you put some apples (both green and red varieties) on the altar. You can arrange them so that they are tumbling out of a beautiful harvest basket. Then as you begin telling the story of Adam and Eve, walk over to the altar and pick up an apple. Several times during the message, stop and take a bite out of the apple, giving yourself plenty of time to chew it. Don't say a word about why you are eating the apple or try to explain yourself. Just do it without explanation. The congregation will understand your action, and it will add depth to the words you are speaking. Don't forget to smile when you see their surprised faces.

EXTRAS:

Try creating an apple scent in your sanctuary for this message. You can do this with a few well-placed apple-scented candles. Be sure to put the scent in the narthex or gathering place as well.

If you want, you can have the ushers carry in the basket of apples to start the service. They can walk up to the altar and pour the basket out on its side, positioning the apples so they don't fall off, and then walk out. This gesture will increase the level of curiosity in the room.

ENDING:

Before the benediction, walk over to the altar and dramatically put down the chewed-up apple.

A LEAN AND A LIMP
Jacob's Ladder

Genesis 32:22–32

THE MESSAGE:

1. As my kids are starting to head out into the world on their own, I'm conscious of the things I'll greatly miss. I'll miss Sara being near me to fix everything that breaks and to give me sweet words of understanding and encouragement. I'll miss Andrew's hugs and kisses and the way he believes in me and in everything I do. And, I'll miss Natalie's lean. My middle child is now a teenager, but she still leans on me when she walks beside me. When we go to the mall, because our walking patterns are so similar, we walk smoothly beside each other, and she always gently leans into me as she walks. I'll miss that. (Of course, I'd prefer if you found your own "leaning" story as a substitute to mine!)

2. Describe Jacob's wrestling match with God. His hip was touched, and as a result he walked with a limp from thereon, leaning on God as his crutch. Remember all that Jacob had to learn through Esau's forgiveness when he came home. Remember how he so bravely (ha!) sent the women and children ahead of him to meet Esau after the years of misunderstanding. And remember the way he was persistent in getting a blessing, a touch, from God.

3. "Many fans, few friends." I heard a speaker at a conference say that he had "many fans but few friends." He traveled for

a living, speaking in many cities. Therefore he didn't have time to develop close relationships with family and friends. This grieved him. It was his limp and it made him lean.

4. Describe a person who struggles with a physical disability and yet does great things for God. I told the story of Doris, a woman with beautiful white hair and a walker, who pushed herself along and led a Bible study group, even though walking was difficult for her. She did what she could with what she had.

5. Now tell about your own lean and limp. And encourage the people to name *their* leans and limps. See how God is with us in the lean and the limp of life! Thanks be to God.

THE BACKGROUND:

Jacob was going home. Do you remember the circumstances surrounding his leaving? He had tricked his aging father and had stolen the birthright and the blessing from his brother, and so he had to run away to save his life. After twenty years, he was finally going home.

The wrestling occurred as he went home to face his brother, whom he had betrayed. But the one he had to wrestle with was not his brother but God. When he received a blow to his hip, even though it was painful, he still hung on to his need for God's presence. He didn't let go through the pain.

And so, things changed in Jacob's life. Esau met him with reconciliation in his heart. His family found a new home. And God remained faithful. Yet Jacob, left with a limp, never forgot what it cost him or how much he needed God in his life.

THE CREATIVE AVENUE:

This again is a simple movement of the body that will illustrate a position in life: the lean and the limp. I used this phrase "a lean and a limp" throughout the message. The repetitive phrase has power all on its own. There are times in our lives when we recognize that we need to lean on God because we have been hurt or have a limping view.

Every time I said "a lean and a limp," I did a leaning movement with my body, followed immediately by dragging one leg along. You'll have to practice this to get it to come naturally when you say the words. Find a way that is your own style of leaning and limping. It helps to spend some time with God remembering all the ways you have struggled and developed a limp and all the times God has helped you along by allowing you to lean on the everlasting arms of God's grace.

EXTRAS:

I can imagine Jacob needing a walking stick for support after his encounter with the angel. If you want, you can use a walking stick to help you show the "lean and limp" of Jacob's walk.

ENDING:

This is a great place for an old favorite hymn, "Leaning on the Everlasting Arms." Or another favorite song is "Lean on Me," sung between God and the community.

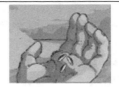

HUNGRY

Psalm 34

Taste and see that the LORD is good. (Ps. 34:8)

For Abby

THE MESSAGE:

1. Introduce to the congregation a chef, and tell a little of his or her story and experience.

2. Tell about your most delicious dining experience ever. Describe in detail the setting, the taste of the food, the company.

3. America has a new problem: we are gaining weight as a country at the same time that we are spending less time eating together. Perhaps what we are hungry for is the connectedness that comes when families eat together.

4. Tell the story of David. Worried because of his enemy Abimelech, David pretends to be insane. This story is the setting for Psalm 34.

5. We all have times of acute hunger and thirst for God, times when we really need God's presence and attention. Tell of a time when you experienced this need.

6. Finish telling David's story, remembering to include how he came to reconnect with his family and with God, to the point that he could praise God by saying, "Taste and see that the Lord is good."

7. Describe the sacrament of Holy Communion and the taste of grace that comes in this moment of forgiveness and renewal.

8. Invite people to the table of Holy Communion.

THE BACKGROUND:

Psalm 34 is a writing that refers to 1 Samuel 21:10–15. David had many enemies and many trials in life. He struggled with his enemies and even with his family. David had a great life, but it was also a hard one. He had people who loved him and were faithful to him as well as people who hated him and betrayed him. He made many mistakes, including adultery and even setting up someone for murder. Yet he had a heart for God. He repented with his whole heart, and when he was cleansed from his sin, he was able to praise God with all of his heart and soul.

When we are forgiven much, we love much, and so David was able to love the Lord even more because of his mistakes. For this reason, he was able to reach the point where he said that God's love *tastes* good! Oh that we can praise like that!

THE CREATIVE AVENUE:

Rev. Tim Wright came up with this idea (thanks, Timoteo!). He set up a cooking station on the platform, and Chef Jeff McCarty made a delicious meal while Tim was talking. Next to the cooking station was a table beautifully set with china and crystal.

If you have a small enough space, you will not only enjoy watching a chef create a wonderful meal, but your taste buds and sense of smell will be filled with delicious aromas. Even if your area is large, imagination will probably help to make people a little hungry.

Have the chef cook while you speak. Introduce him or her, and give some background (education, place of work, specialty meals, etc.). The chef will continue to cook throughout the remainder of the message.

Set up a cue easily recognized by the chef so that when you are nearing the end of your sermon, he or she can set the food on the table and sit down to eat just as you are ending.

EXTRAS:

At your entryway into the church (narthex or lobby), have a large table set with beautiful china and accessories you might see at a holiday meal. It will peak interest and cause folks to wonder what will happen in the service.

ENDING:

Enjoy your Sunday lunch! Enjoy your life in Christ! Bon appétit!

FEATHERS

Psalm 91:4

THE MESSAGE:

1. Describe how children are more carefree than adults because they have trust in their parents' protection. For example, my kids used to sit on my lap and then suddenly throw their head and body backward, confident that Mommy would catch them. Children are delightfully free to dance and laugh and have greater joy because they have experienced safety and protection. Only as we grow older and experience pain does this freedom fade.

2. The scripture says that God is our protector and that "He will shelter you with His feathers." Describe how feathers protect the tender skin of a bird. God's intent is to protect us like feathers protect a bird.

3. Now talk about the opposite: the times when we feel fearful and unprotected and when we doubt God's protection from disaster.

4. Tell a story about a time when it was obvious that God protected you.

5. Discuss God's desire to protect us even when we can't see it or don't understand what is happening to us.

6. "Light as a feather" is a phrase that describes a person of little weight, but it is often used to describe when a weight or burden has been lifted from our souls.

7. As you finish this sequence, walk to the basket of feathers, take a handful, and toss them into the air, saying, "You are free because God is watching out for you!"

THE BACKGROUND:

Feathers are unique to birds. They have many functions including:

1. Keeping the body warm

2. Helping with flying

3. Giving color

4. Providing contour, which shapes the individual look of the bird

Feathers are made of the protein keratin (the protein found in hair), and the lightweight form of a feather enables flight to occur (imagine how difficult it would be to fly if the feathers were heavier). Feathers protect, keep warm, aid in flight, and provide beautiful coloring.[33]

Some fun facts about feathers are:

• The ruby-throated hummingbird, at a count of 940 feathers, has the least feathers.

• The whistling swan has the most feathers (needs more protection from cold winters).

• The longest feather in the world is from an ornamental chicken that was bred in Japan. This feather is 34.75 feet long!

THE CREATIVE AVENUE:

Find a down (feather) pillow, and cut it open. Fill a basket with feathers, and place it in a prominent place, but not at the altar. At the end of the sermon, talk about how God protects us as feathers protect birds. Say something like, "Be free, because God is protecting you!" As you say this, take a handful of feathers and toss them into the air. The larger the handful, the greater the effect. You will sense a whimsical nature of freedom as you see the feathers float to the ground.

This will certainly make a mess, so be prepared. Also, some people are allergic to down feathers so be sure to take this into consideration.

EXTRAS:

Provide each person with a feather as a memory of the message. You can pass out a small feather as people enter or you can tape a feather to each bulletin.

ENDING:

Be silent as you watch the feathers float to the ground. As they begin to reach the floor, lead the people in a prayer that they would know God's freedom and protection.

THANKFUL
Thanksgiving Sunday

Colossians 2:6–7

THE MESSAGE:

The theme of this message is simple: be thankful for all that God has done for you, and let your thankfulness overflow to those around you. Gratefulness is the state of the heart most pleasing to God. Gratefulness occurs when we recognize our status as forgiven and renewed, when we recognize our need for God's faithfulness in our lives, and when we have such joy that it can't help but spill over and influence others. This is the rooted and grounded faith of a thankful heart.

The parts of this message could be as follows:

1. Tell about a time when you were truly grateful for something in your life. It could be when you got married or had a baby, or when someone helped you cope with a difficult situation. Let your story show heartfelt thanks.

2. Thanksgiving traditions. Discuss the various traditions of Thanksgiving, including some historical background.

3. Expound on the scripture passage. It is interesting to note that a grateful life comes out of obedience, rootedness, nourishment in faith, and staying in the truth that we were taught. From this we find that our hearts are overflowing with thanks for all that God has done. The passage seems to be saying that the deeper we are, the more grateful we will become.

4. The tradition of five kernels. Tell of this Thanksgiving tradition (see THE BACKGROUND). At our dinner table on Thanksgiving, we would each have five kernels on our dinner plate. We would pass around a basket, and each person would tell what they were thankful for and then put the kernels in the basket. This basket was then set in the middle of the dinner table as a reminder. Then we would wipe away the tears, hope the food was still warm, pray, and eat!

5. Invite the people to bring one kernel to the altar and pause for a prayer of thanks to God. Then encourage them to take the four remaining kernels and pass them out to the people in their lives for whom they are thankful, stopping to tell each person exactly why they are grateful.

THE BACKGROUND:

The Thanksgiving kernel tradition dates back to the year 1621 when the Pilgrims endured one of the harshest winters. The people were cold and starving due to a lack of resources. According to tradition, the people were so hungry that at one point, they were given only five kernels of corn on their plates! Later a ship came in, and they were able to trade fur pelts for corn. Placing five kernels of corn on the Thanksgiving dinner plate is a way to remember God's past goodness during a hard time.[34]

I encourage you to tell a few additional Thanksgiving Day stories. You can find specific stories about this holiday on the Internet or at your library.

THE CREATIVE AVENUE:

Each person will be given four kernels of corn (popcorn works great). The best way is to have baskets of kernels for the ushers to pass out to each person as they enter. You will get questions about the corn ("What's this for?"), so instruct ushers to say that it's for the sermon. This will heighten the sense of awareness and surprise as people wonder what's coming up.

During the message, tell the story of the Pilgrims and the kernels of corn. Show your handful of kernels as you tell this story.

At the end of the message, invite the people to come forward and lay one kernel on the altar or some area in the front of the sanctuary. As they do this, have them say a prayer of thanks to God for something God has done for them. Be sure to leave enough time in the service for people to come forward. Then ask everyone to take the final four kernels and pass them out to people during the week, telling why they are thankful for each person.

We also taped up large sheets of butcher paper on the walls of the sanctuary. We provided pens (be sure they don't leak through to your walls) and asked the people to write what they are thankful for on the paper. This was done in the beginning of the service, during the time when we were singing a set of songs. Display the paper the following week.

EXTRAS:

- Decorate the altar with a horn of plenty, fruit, corn, and wheat tares.
- Choose songs that sing of a grateful heart.
- During the children's moment, tell the Thanksgiving story, and let the children tell you what they are thankful for this year.

ENDING:

Have the people stand and hold hands to represent the community of God. Pray for them and for the ability to live grateful lives.

ABOUT THE SAINTS
All Saints' Sunday

2 Timothy 1:5–7

THE MESSAGE:

This is a sermon to remember and honor the saints of old who brought us up in faith. It reminds us that we are not alone and that those who have gone before us have taught us well. It allows us, for a moment, to lean back into the arms of those who have loved us and have spoken to us about the way God loves us too.

1. Describe someone who has passed on into eternity. Tell how that person taught you about God's love. I talked about my grandma, who used to have her Bible on her lap as she sat in her easy chair. I'd ask her what she was reading, and she would tell me some of her thoughts. As a special birthday gift, my mom gave my grandma's Bible to me, and it holds special memories.

2. Tell the story of Timothy, a young man who was mentored by the apostle Paul as well as by his mother and grandmother. These two women must have had incredible faith because Paul encourages Timothy to remain in the tradition of his mom and grandma!

3. Mentoring. Talk about how we learn from our mentors. The process of life is to have a mentor and to be a mentor. Mentoring is one of the best ways of learning. Often our mentors' actions tell us so much more than their words could ever say.

4. Death as a window to heaven. When we sit beside someone who is dying, we get an unusual glimpse into heaven. For a moment we can imagine heaven and see what it might be like for our loved one as they enter. As pastors, we see this more often than most. And we can remember many times when the person who is dying describes a light or speaks to someone who has passed on before them or says some parting words of forgiveness and love. Tell some of those stories.

5. Death is not the end. What we have learned and how we have been loved do not stop when someone dies. We carry within us the genes of their sacrifices. We hold their DNA. Our words of hope come from their examples of courage. The ones who have gone to eternity are still connected to us and still inform us, and for that we are grateful.

6. Invite people to remember someone who has died. Be gentle with this invitation, speaking of the memory in positive ways. Then invite them to light a candle in honor of their beloved. Have some musicians play a song during this time of movement.

7. As they return to their seats, remind the congregation that they are the mentors for the next generation and that they have a story to tell and love to give.

THE BACKGROUND:

Timothy is a name that means "honored of God." He was from Lystra, a city in Asia Minor. He became a close associate of the apostle Paul and traveled with him to the areas of Thessalonica, Macedonia, Corinth, and Ephesus. We know that Timothy's father was Greek and that his mother and grandmother, Eunice and Lois, were Jewish. This means that his grandfather was not very orthodox because he allowed his daughter to be married to a man who was not Jewish. Timothy, therefore, was uncircumcised. But his mother, Eunice, was a follower of the Jewish faith, and Paul commends her and her mother, Lois, for that faith. Paul points out that they raised Timothy in the ways of God.

Timothy received two letters from Paul, 1 and 2 Timothy.[35] When Paul wrote 2 Timothy, he was on death row, and he wrote the letter to encourage Timothy to keep on in the faith. This letter has much to say about how Christians can believe and can act out their beliefs.[36]

THE CREATIVE AVENUE:

The creative action of this message is to invite people to light a candle to represent someone they love who has passed on. Set up a tiered stand that can hold many small votive candles. The tiered effect lets you see every light and adds depth to the visual. You will need four to six stands, depending on the size of your congregation. Light a few of the candles. Place wooden skewers so that people can light a candle from an existing flame.

During the sermon, wherever you want to place this action, invite the people to light a candle. Provide background music during this time. Have enough candles and stations for everyone to light a candle. If you have a large congregation, you will need many stations so that you don't hamper the flow of the people or create long lines. We were surprised to see how the congregation responded to this movement. They were deeply touched to be able to remember a loved one.

EXTRAS:

Provide something they can take with them to remember their loved ones. For example, a crystal rock (sold in craft stores) or a small cross will do. Put these near the candles so that the people can easily take one after they light a candle.

ENDING:

During the benediction, remind people that they are the light of the world (gesture to the candles) and that it is their turn to take that light out to their world.

LOOKING FORWARD
New Year's Sunday

Philippians 3:12–14

THE MESSAGE:

1. Put it behind you. Tell of a time when you needed to put something behind you, walk away, and not look back but instead remember what you have learned and go forward. When I left my last church, I had to do that. I had to remember what I had learned and all the wonderful ways God had changed me while I was there. But as I walked away, I was missing the people in the congregation and I found myself pining for them, wishing I could still be with them. But I knew that I was called to face forward, so I had a wrestling match with God. The result was that I knew I had to set it behind me. It was more difficult than I am making it sound—in fact, it broke my heart. I will always remember them with great love, but I know that they are in God's hands and that now my journey is going a different direction. So I had to make myself face forward in faith.

2. Discuss the scripture passage. Paul talks about keeping on— pressing forward and not giving up. He recognizes that he has not reached a state of perfection and that there is room for growth. He admits to his failings. But he reminds us to focus on two things: (1) forgetting the past, and (2) looking to the future. It takes work to do both. Sometimes we have to work hard to keep putting down what is in our past. Our human

inclination is to keep picking up the stuff we have determined to set aside. And it takes focus to keep looking forward and to keep reminding ourselves of the goal. We have to tell ourselves every day what we are working toward. It takes energy—even straining—to go forward in life. The first thing we must do is to put something behind.

3. Ask the people to write down on the first piece of paper something from the past year they want to leave behind at the cross. Invite them to bring their pieces of paper to the cross (see THE CREATIVE AVENUE).

4. Talk about a time when you strained forward to reach a goal. For me, this was when I ran a marathon. At about mile twenty, I was ready to forget it all. My feet were tired, my body ached, and my mind was weak. All I wanted was a cool shower and a soft bed. But pushing through the "wall" of a marathon was one of the most powerful moments of my life. When I crossed the finish line, I knew that I had completed a goal with the help of God. And it was worth the pain.

5. Now invite the congregation to a time of reflection in which they write down on the second piece of paper the things they want to look forward to this year.

6. Talk about Paul's position in life when he wrote this letter (see THE BACKGROUND).

7. Encourage the people to keep going forward in the new year, to not ever give up, and to strain toward the prize.

THE BACKGROUND:

Paul wrote this epistle when he was in prison. It is quite amazing how someone could have such clarity and could focus on the joy of the Lord during one of the hardest times in his life. While he was writing about joy in Christ, Paul was facing his own execution. We know that when people face hard times, they are sometimes able to take the high road, as was the case for Paul. He encouraged the people of Philippi to live as Christ lived, to be humble and honest, and to keep high standards. He reminded them to be content with their lives and to love whatever is noble, true, just, pure, and lovely. He spoke of the beauty of being in Christ at a time when he was surrounded by a great amount of filth, injustice, and poverty of spirit. In the darkest days of his life, he encouraged followers of Christ to start new and to press on.

THE CREATIVE AVENUE:

Put a large cross in a prominent position in your sanctuary.

As people enter, pass out two 3′ X 5′ cards to each person (you can have the ushers pass them out or put them in the bulletins).

In the first half of the sermon, you will invite the people to write on one card the things they want to leave behind. Then they will bring that card and lay it at the foot of the cross.

In the second half of the message, ask the people to write on the second card what they are looking forward to this year. Ask them to take this card home and to look at it once a month throughout the year.

EXTRAS:

If you have a newborn baby in the congregation, have the parents lift up that child as a symbol of new life on this New Year's Sunday.

ENDING:

During the benediction, have the people hold their cards up, and give a blessing that encourages them to look forward to the goal.

THIRTY-EIGHT SEEDS

MAMA
Mother's Day Sunday

Psalm 139:13–17

THE MESSAGE:

This message is written from a mother's perspective. The theme is that God formed us while we were in our mothers' wombs. The womb is a place of protection, nourishment, and connection. God cherishes the child by choosing the mother's womb to show God's love.

1. Tell a story of the miracle of life within the womb. The story I tell is the one my mother told me about my time in her womb. She says that every time she stepped into a church, I would start flipping around inside her. I made her nauseous with my activity in church. She said that she wondered at times if she could even make it through one more Sunday with me inside her. And when I was outside of her womb and in her arms, Mama always told me that I had a connection to God (as shown by my love of church in utero) that would stay with me my whole life. No wonder I became a pastor!

2. Describe the miracle of babies being formed in utero (see THE BACKGROUND).

3. Discuss the scripture passage, emphasizing that God knew us even in the womb. He chose our mothers to carry us and was intimately involved in every part of our formation and our mothers' care during this time.

4. Tell how God provided us with a mother's protective loving care after our births. If possible, use a story from your own life. My own mother was great at giving me hugs after school every day. I always knew I could count on her hugs. And she had many encouraging words for me along the journey of my life. She lifted me up and understood me. In my darkest moment, my mother spoke hope and life to me.

5. Now remind the women of your congregation that all women have a "mothering" role. This opens up the discussion to include those women who do not or cannot have children. Also speak for a moment to those people who have painful memories of their mothers, and remind them that God has sent them other "mothers" and that God Herself will be their Mother.

6. Remember the well-known mothers in the Bible, including Eve, Sarah, Rebecca, Ruth, Hannah, Mary, Lois, and Eunice. Remember how they shaped the course of history by their love for God and for their communities.

7. Have the women stand. Have the congregation reach out their hands to touch the women and lead them in a blessing.

THE BACKGROUND:

In the Scripture, David has a message of great joy. He speaks about the fact that God goes everywhere David goes. There is no place David can go that God is not! Even in his mother's womb, God is there protecting, forming, and dreaming for him.

Our mothers are like that. They know us. They seem to have "eyes in the back of their heads" sometimes. Even when we think they don't know what we are doing, they do. Your mother is your guide, your foundation, and your protective environment for life. Love her well because she has done an amazing job shaping your life!

Some of the miracles inside the womb:

- **Week 4**—The blastocyst anchors itself in the uterine wall and is just a tiny speck of living matter.

- **Week 6**—The baby is the size of a lentil and has cardiac muscles and a beating heart. The heart is the first organ to function.

- **Week 8**—The baby grows to the size of a lima bean and floats in the amniotic fluid. The esophagus forms, and the buds of lungs appear.

- **Week 18**—The baby has fingerprints and can be seen sucking her thumb.

- **Week 21**—The baby has sleep patterns, and a mom can tell when baby is sleeping and when he is awake.

- **Week 27**—The baby can open her eyes and look around. Eyelashes grow.

- **Week 30**—The baby weighs three pounds and is covered with downy hair.

- **Birth**—The baby has gained weight and is fully functioning outside of the mother's womb.[37]

THE CREATIVE AVENUE:

Ask the women and the men to sit in church as people did in New Testament days. Move the women (children can go with them) to one side of the church and the men to the other. When you speak, look at the women as often as you can, giving them preference on this day.

Most people will be hesitant to move out of their seats. Just let them know that they are sitting in seats of honor this Sunday. As they move, have the men pass out a carnation, or other symbol, to each girl and woman present.

Then at the end of the message, have the men go and stand by the women to give them a prayer of blessing.

EXTRAS:

Have the children prepare for this day by making Mother's Day cards for the whole congregation.

Ask a group of daughters (teens work well) to sing a special song for this day.

ENDING:

Call the women to continue to protect, nurture, and form the generations and the people God has placed in their lives.

DADDY
Father's Day Sunday

Psalm 103:13–18

THE MESSAGE:

Father's Day is when we stop and look at our dads and thank God for them. Today we will look at fathers and at our heavenly Father and see what they have in common.

1. Describe your dad, or the person who related to you as a father. This was easy for me. My dad was a man who listened to me, asked me questions about my thoughts, discussed theology with me, and lived his life in the active stance of serving God. He was my rock and my foundation, and he made my life better just by being in the same house. I loved his humor and his subtle way of engaging whoever was in the room.

2. Recognize that some people have difficulty with their fathers. They may see them as harsh, absent, abusive, or lacking understanding. Recognize this pain that exists in our society.

3. Now look at the scripture. In this psalm the author says that God is "like a father to his children" and then describes the behavior of a father as "tender and compassionate." God understands our weakness. His love remains forever, no matter where the winds blow.

4. Call the fathers in the congregation to become this kind of father, one that is called "tender" and "compassionate" and "faithful." Challenge your fathers to stand up to this call. They

may have made some mistakes along the way, but today is a new day. Let them know they can be the kind of father that God is.

5. Tell a story about a father that made a difference.

6. Tell the story of the origin of Father's Day (see THE BACKGROUND).

THE BACKGROUND:

The celebration of Father's Day began when Sonora Dodd wanted to honor her father, William Smart. Her mother had died giving birth to her sixth child, and Mr. Smart was left to raise six children alone. They lived on a rural farm in Washington State, so life wasn't easy by any means. After Sonora became an adult, she realized how much it took for her father to raise her family alone and wanted a day to honor him as a courageous and loving father. She spoke to her pastor, and they dedicated Sunday June 19 as Father's Day. Sonora wore a red rose to honor her dad during his life, and a white rose to honor him after his death. In 1924 President Calvin Coolidge made the third Sunday in June a day to honor fathers, and in 1966 President Lyndon Johnson signed a presidential proclamation to that effect.[38]

THE CREATIVE AVENUE:

This simple creative sermon provides a way for sons and daughters to tell their fathers that they love them. You do this by giving them an assignment.

Provide each person with a river rock (get them in bulk at craft stores). Ask each person to write their name on one side of the rock with permanent markers. On the other side, write one word that reminds them of the essence of their father (the word might be "honor," or "faithful," or "humor," or "loving"). Then ask them to take time to deliver (or mail) this rock to their dad. If he is far away, a phone call to explain the rock will suffice. Encourage them to take this assignment as a chance to let their dads know how much they mean to them.

Some people truly can't do this because of troubled childhoods. In their cases, if they can't approach their dads, then have them present the rock to another person in their lives who acted as a father figure. For those who have no one but their heavenly Father, invite them to present their rock to God at the altar.

EXTRAS:

Give the fathers present (I like to include all males as "father figures" and "fathers-to-be") a gift such as a red carnation (cheaper than roses), a pen, or a rock in the shape of a heart (search your craft shops for this). Having something tangible for them to take home and to touch will remind them of the many ways they are loved.

ENDING:

Have the fathers, and all the boys and men, stand up while you lead the congregation in giving them a blessing, calling them to be tender, compassionate, and faithful members of their families.

FREE INDEED
Fourth of July Sunday

John 8:31–37; 1 Kings 3:16–28

THE MESSAGE:

1. A Christian disciple. In this passage of scripture, Jesus reminds the people to keep obeying His teachings. That implies not only knowing God's teachings, but also acting on that knowledge. To obey is to do something about what we know. The result of this is knowing the truth! And we all want to know the truth about the situations in our lives. We want the truth because we know the truth will set us free.

2. Tell the story of Solomon's needing to know the truth about who was the mother of the baby left alive (see 1 Kings 3:16–28).

3. Back to Jesus. Reading this passage is like listening to an argument between Jesus and the religious leaders. When Jesus told them that the truth would "set them free," they were irate! This phrase carried some baggage with it. In their history, they had endured slavery in Egypt and had received God's promise never to be slaves of anyone again (Lev. 25:39–42). That's why the Jewish leaders were always saying they were accountable first to God and were not slaves to any government they happened to be under. Josephus, a Jewish historian who lived in the first century CE, said this of the Jews: "They have an inviolable attachment to liberty, and they say that God is to be their only Ruler and Lord."[39] So the Jewish leaders

were totally offended by Jesus' use of the phrase "you will be set free," because they were already free!

4. Americans and freedom. Freedom is one of our nation's core values as well. Like the Jewish leaders of Jesus' day, we bristle if someone tells us that we are not free. Freedom is guaranteed by our Constitution and Bill of Rights, we fight wars for freedom, and, most important, freedom is written on our hearts. Americans love freedom.

We operate out of the "Don't mess with me; I'm a free human being" mentality. We have the "Don't touch this!" perspective if anyone messes with our core value of freedom. Just like the Jewish leaders of Jesus' day.

5. Freedom from sin. Jesus was talking about the ultimate freedom: being free from sin. If we are slaves to sin, then we are not free. So, who among us can experience this ultimate freedom, the freedom from sin? Who is perfect, righteous, and holy? Who is pure, clean, and innocent? Jesus gives the promise, *"So if the Son sets you free, you will indeed be free"* (John 8:36).

6. Some related scripture:
    a. *"For you, dear friends, have been called to live in freedom—not freedom to satisfy your sinful nature, but freedom to serve one another in love"* (Gal. 5:13).
    b. *"Don't you realize that whatever you choose to obey becomes your master? . . . Now you are free from sin, your old master, and you have become slaves to your new master, righteousness"* (Rom. 6:16, 18).
    c. *"So now there is no condemnation for those who belong to Christ Jesus. For the power of the life-giving Spirit has freed you through Christ Jesus from the power of sin that leads to death"* (Rom. 8:1–2).
    d. *"Those who are dominated by the sinful nature think about sinful things, but those who are controlled by the Holy Spirit think about things that please the Spirit. If your sinful nature controls your mind, there is death. But if the Holy Spirit controls your mind, there is life and peace"* (Rom. 8:5–6).

7. Independence Day. It's Independence Day, a national holiday. Live for Christ, free from the control of sin, and you will be truly free.

THE BACKGROUND:

Being a part of a people bound by slavery changes you. Your ancestors have gone through something awful, and yet they rose up and liberated themselves. Because of their previous bondage, freedom is more precious to them than it is to those who have never experienced slavery. And when your family has fought to be free from control, you will passionately raise the banner for ongoing freedom. You won't let yourself go back. That's how the Jewish people felt. They had been slaves in Egypt, and God had rescued them even in the face of the great Pharaoh! They had survived his torture and then survived the torture of wandering around in the desert for forty years. They weren't going back there again. No more leeks, no more being overworked, no more manna, no more desert heat, no more homelessness. They thought they were already free, so when Jesus said, "The truth will set you free," they were offended! As Americans who value freedom as a right, we can understand their perspective.

THE CREATIVE AVENUE:

I start out this message by showing how I can cross each finger on top of the other (a childlike game we used to play). You may want to begin with something similar. Then ask the people to cross some part of their body, if they are able, and to hold that position until you tell them to uncross themselves. They may want to cross their feet, their ankles, their legs, their arms, or their fingers.

In the beginning this is an easy task, but after a while it becomes hard to remain still. You begin to feel some aches and pains from limited movement. That's the point: to help people feel what it is like *not* to be free!

EXTRAS:

It's Independence Day, so celebrate this in your service. I like to have people who have fought for our freedom stand (identify each branch of the Armed Forces separately) and let the congregation express gratitude to them.

This is a great time to sing songs of freedom and to have a group present the colors.

ENDING:

Ask the congregation to uncross their limbs. Then say "Ah . . . ! It feels good to be free, free indeed!"

Notes

[1] Kathleen M. O'Connor, "The Book of Lamentations," *The New Interpreter's Bible*, vol. 6 (Nashville: Abingdon Press, 2001), 1023.

[2] See the chapters on Jeremiah in *The Word in Life Study Bible*, New King James Version (Nashville: Thomas Nelson, 1993).

[3] Read *The Imagineering Way: Ideas to Ignite Your Creativity* (New York: Disney Editions, 2003).

[4] Scott Thorpe, *How to Think Like Einstein, Simple Ways to Break the Rules and Discover Your Hidden Genius* (Naperville, IL: Sourcebooks, 2000), 60.

[5] Frederick A. Norwood, *The Story of American Methodism* (Nashville: Abingdon Press, 1974), 15–41.

[6] Chad Brand, Charles Draper, and Archie England, eds., *Holman Illustrated Bible Dictionary* (Nashville: Holman Bible Publishers, 2003), 1550–52, 1560–68.

[7] See http://www.gracehappens.org.

[8] See books by Leonard Sweet and Brian McLaren.

[9] William Barclay, *The Gospel of Mark*, The New Daily Study Bible (Philadelphia: Westminster John Knox Press, 2001).

[10] Frederick Buechner, *Wishful Thinking: A Theological ABC* (New York: Harper & Row, 1973).

[11] Ronald F. Youngblood, F. F. Bruce, and R. K. Harrison, *Nelson's New Illustrated Bible Dictionary* (Nashville: Thomas Nelson, 1995), 459.

[12] William Barclay, *The Gospel of John*, vol. 1, The Daily Study Bible (Philadelphia: Westminster John Knox Press, 1975), 95–99.

[13] I heard this story along the way but cannot recall its original souce. For documentation, do a Google or Yahoo search on these words (include quote marks): "long walk part of gift."

[14] See Merriam-Webster OnLine. http://www.merriam-webster.com/

[15] W. E. Vine, *Vine's Concise Dictionary of Bible Words*, *Nelson's Concise Series* (Nashville: Nelson Reference, 1999), 334.

[16] William Barclay, *The Letters to the Corinthians*, The Daily Study Bible (Philadelphia: Westminster John Knox Press, 1975), 1–5.

[17] See http://www.earlychristianwritings.com/text/actspaul.html (accessed July 28, 2005).

[18] See http://www.whfoods.com/genpage.php?tname=food-spice&dbid=106 (accessed July 28, 2005).

[19] See http://www.cbsnews.com/stories/2004/10/01/60minutes/main646890.shtml (accessed July 28, 2005).

[20] Elizabeth McCardell, review of *Adult Crying, A Biophychosocial Approach*, ed. J. J. M. Vingerhoets and Randolph R. Cornelius, *Human Nature Review* 3 (March 22, 2003), 219–221. See also http://human-nature.com/nibbs/03/crying.html (accessed March 30, 2005).

[21] See the Singapore Science Centre Web site: http://www.science.edu.sg/ssc/detailed.jsp?artid=5147&type=6&roo (accessed March 30, 2005).

[22] For more information or to purchase tear bottles, see http://www.timelesstraditionsgifts.com/tearbott.htm (accessed March 30, 2005).

[23] See http://www.lachrymatory.com/History.htm (accessed March 30, 2005).

[24] Brand, Draper, and England, *Holman Illustrated Bible Dictionary*, 50–51.

[25] Josephine Cutts and James Smith, *Essential Van Gogh* (New York: Barnes & Noble Books, 2001).

[26] Antonia Cunningham and Karen Hurrell, *Essential Impressionists* (New York: Barnes & Noble Books, 2001).

[27] Kristen Bradbury, Antonia Cunningham, Lucinda Hawksley, and Laura Payne, *Essential History of Art* (New York: Barnes & Noble Books, 2001).

[28] Brand, Draper, and England, *Holman Illustrated Bible Dictionary*.

[29] *Word-in-Life Study Bible*, 148.

[30] Youngblood, Bruce, and Harrison, *Nelson's New Illustrated Bible Dictionary*, 392–94.

[31] Ibid., 368.

[32] Brand, Draper, and England, *Holman Illustrated Bible Dictionary*, 25-26.

[33] See these Web pages about bird feathers:

"The Wonder of Bird Feathers,"
http://www.earthlife.net/birds/feathers.html (accessed April 20, 2005).

"Feathers," http://fsc.fernbank.edu/Birding/feathers.htm (accessed April 20, 2005).

[34] Barbara Rainey. "A Thanksgiving Tradition." *Worldwide Challenge* 29, no. 6 (November/Dececember 2003), http://www.wwc-magazine.org/2003/novdec034.html (accessed April 23, 2005).

[35] *The Word in Life Study Bible*, New King James Version (Nashville: Thomas Nelson, 1993), 2194–96.

[36] John Drane, ed., "Timothy," *Encyclopedia of the Bible*. (Nashville: Thomas Nelson, 2001), 267.

[37] Parents.com magazine. "The Inside Story, Fetal Development Weeks 1-4" http://www.parents.com/articles/pregnancy/1029.jsp (accessed April 23, 2005).

See also the articles on Weeks 5–8, Weeks 18–21, and Weeks 27–30.

[38] "History of Father's Day." http://www.twilightbridge.com-/hobbies/festivals/father/history.html (accessed April 24, 2005).

[39] William Barclay, *The Gospel of John*, The Daily Study Bible. (This whole section is based on the writings of Barclay.)